Home Brewing with BeerSmith ™

How to Brew and Design Great Beer at Home

Bradley J Smith, PhD
Author, Brewer, Engineer

BeerSmith.com
BeerSmith LLC

Published by:
BeerSmith LLC
Clifton, Virginia 20124

BeerSmith ™ is a trademark of BeerSmith LLC

ISBN: 1453851496

EAN-13: 9781453851494

Dedication

This book is dedicated to my wife and children who have been inspiring, supportive and patient with my writing and entrepreneurial journey these past 7 years.

Table of Contents

Introduction

My personal home brewing adventure started in 1987 in the kitchen of my small apartment. Hunched over Charlie Papazian's book <u>The Joy of Homebrewing</u>, I brewed my first beer.

It was not a particularly good beer, and I recall several bottles from my second beer exploded in the kitchen one day making quite a mess. But I managed to stay with it, and enjoyed creating new brews. Things got much easier in the 1990's when liquid yeast and better quality ingredients arrived.

Sometime in 2002, I was frustrated trying to keep good records for my recipes, and started writing a little program to manage my beer records. About a year later I published my BeerSmith beer brewing software, not knowing it would later become quite popular.

In 2003, I also established **BeerSmith.com**, and a discussion forum (**forum.beersmith.com**) where I made a number of great brewing friends. Over time I experimented with a number of other sites including a Wiki (**brewwiki.com**), and news site (**brewpoll.com**) to help serve and expand the brewing community with varying degrees of success.

In 2008 I started writing short articles on beer brewing weekly for the BeerSmith blog (**blog.beersmith.com**). After six months and dozens of articles, I had less than 100 subscribers and was ready to give up. However in the past two years that number has expanded into several thousand, and the blog now draws a substantial amount of web traffic.

In early 2010, I passed the "100 article" mark and someone asked me if there was a printed version of the blog. I thought about it for a while, and said why not?

The book you hold in your hands is a collection of beer brewing articles from the BeerSmith blog – but it also embodies much of what I've learned in the last 23+ years of home brewing.

As a collection of articles, it is not perfect – in some areas it jumps topics quickly, but I think you will find much here that is not covered well in other brewing books laid out in an approachable manner – particularly for the intermediate brewer.

I decided to self-publish this book using Amazon's print-on-demand service to allow me to reach you directly. I would like to thank the Lee Morse, Richard Lane of Carolina Brewmasters, and Mark Skrainer of the Brewing Network who voluntarily took on a role as editors for this book – their help has been invaluable:

Thank you also to DJ Speiss of **Fermentarium.com** who provided the fine article on Kolsch.

I hope you will enjoy reading the book as much as I have enjoyed writing and participating in the brewing community these past years. I continue to write weekly, so please don't hesitate to visit my blog at **blog.beersmith.com** to get my latest articles, give our BeerSmith software a spin, subscribe to my newsletter, or see what happens next!

Happy Brewing!

Brad Smith, PhD – BeerSmith.com

Twitter: beersmith
Facebook: facebook.com/BeerSmithFans

Chapter 1: Brewing Your First Beer

"He is a wise man who invented beer" --
Plato

Introduction to Brewing

Why start brewing beer at home? Home brewing is both a rewarding and challenging hobby that can be enjoyed with your friends and fellow brewers. The reasons people brew vary tremendously, but brewing beer is a popular hobby. In the United States alone as many as two million people take part in brewing beer at home each year. Some of the advantages of home brewing include:

- **Intrinsic Rewards**- Brewing beer has its own intrinsic value. There is something people find inherently rewarding in the creative process. It's not just any beer, it's your beer that you designed and created with your own two hands. In a sense, the ability to do something new, unusual, challenging and rewarding is the basis for all hobbies including this one.

- **Limited Time Needed** – Brewing is a great hobby for busy people, as it really does not take that much work and time to brew a batch of beer. Extract brewing consumes perhaps a few hours of time spread out over several weeks, and all grain brewing adds only a few hours of additional work. You can adjust the amount of time as needed to match your schedule.

- **Quality over Quantity** – Home brewed beer is hand crafted, which means the home brewer can use ingredients and techniques that are commercially infeasible for the big breweries. In home brewing, all-malt, full-bodied beer is the standard, and cheap additives are the exception.

- **Imagination Unleashed** – Brewing beer opens up a world of possibilities. Home brewers can experiment with ingredients, styles and techniques spanning the entire world. The possibilities are limited only by the brewer's imagination.

- **The Cost Advantage** – Penny pinching all grain home brewers can brew 5 gallons of beer for much less than the cost of comparable high-quality commercial beer.

- **The Social Aspect** – Home brewing is inherently a social hobby. Brewers are passionate about their beer, and the home brewing community is vibrant and growing. In addition, you may find your neighbors are fond of your latest creation and start dropping by more often to sample your beer. The internet and Web 2.0 sites such as our BeerSmith forum at **forum.beersmith.com** let you reach out to brewers from around the world.

- **Health Benefits** – A number of medical studies indicate that alcohol, properly used in moderation at 1-2 drinks per day can provide a number of health benefits. Obviously drinking too much can have a huge negative effect, so I recommend drinking in moderation always. In addition, dark beers provide many of the same benefits as dark wines with regards to high flavinoid content to promote a healthy heart. All natural ingredients including a solid dose of brewer's yeast and vitamin B provide secondary health benefits. A recent article by Charlie Papazian points out that a 12 oz glass of beer has fewer calories than 12 ounces of juice, milk or soda.

- **The Challenge** – Making commercial quality beer at home using recipes you developed is a challenge. However the challenge is part of the charm. There is a wonder in sharing a beer you created by hand with friends that is made even better if it is a difficult style or complex technique. Pushing the limits of the hobby to create the perfect brew is part of the fun.

- **Unlimited Variety** – Home brewing takes us outside the narrow limits of popular commercial beer, and exposes the home brewer to a world of beer styles and possibilities. Home brewed beer gives you the opportunity to explore freshly made German, English, Belgian and other styles that an average beer lover in the US would seldom be able to purchase, especially when fresh and at peak flavor.

Brewing your First Beer at Home

Brewing your first beer at home is not difficult, and the equipment needed is not terribly expensive. To help you understand how easy it is, we're going to jump right in and brew our first beer. We'll go back in later chapters and discuss the finer points of various brewing steps.

Equipment Needed

You don't need a large set of fancy and expensive equipment to brew your first batch of beer. Many brewing supply stores sell starter kits for $75 or less. If you are interested in pursuing the hobby long term, a deluxe brewing kit can be found for less than $150. A number of online stores will even ship the equipment and ingredients directly to your door. It can cost even less if you borrow some or all the equipment from a friend. Here's a summary of what is needed:

- **A Large Pot** – at least 3 gallons in size (11.3 l), though a larger one of 7-9 gallons (26-34 l) will generally result in fewer spills and will allow you to move to all-grain brewing later.
- **Tubing & Clamp** – to siphon and bottle the beer- A 6 foot section of 3/8″ ID food grade plastic tubing will work. Clamps are available at your brew store.
- **Airtight Fermenting Bucket** – a 5 gal (19 l) plastic bucket with lid, or a glass carboy. If you can afford it, purchase a glass carboy or "better carboy" as they are easier to keep

sanitized and don't leak. If you get a glass carboy you may need a large bottle brush to clean it.

- **Air Lock and Stopper** – sized to fit your fermenter.
- **A Bottle Filler** – available from your homebrew supplier – should be sized to fit on the end of your siphon tubing.
- **Thermometer** – A floating thermometer with a range of 32-220 F (0-100 C)
- **Bottle Brush** – While not absolutely required, you usually need a small brush to get your bottles clean.
- **A Bottle Capper** – A hand driven device to cap your bottles also available from your homebrew store.
- **Bottle Caps** – New bottle caps sold at your brewing supplier – you need about 50 caps for a 5 gal batch.
- **A Sanitizing solution** – When beer is being made the sugary solution (called wort) is susceptible to infection, so everything must be sanitized before use. Household bleach can be used, but it must be thoroughly rinsed to prevent contamination. Your brew store may have alternatives such as iodophor and Star-San.
- **Bottles** – To bottle 5 gallons (19 l) of beer, you need approximately 52 standard 12 oz bottles, or just over two cases. Remove the labels from the bottle and clean them thoroughly. Do not use twist off bottles – you must use high quality bottles of the type that require a bottle opener.

Ingredients Needed

The list below assumes you want to brew 5 gallons (19 l) of ale. A 5 gallon batch size, or about 2 cases, is a standard size for home brewers, though advanced brewers will sometimes brew 10 or 15 gallon (37-57 l) batches. Ales are easier to brew than lagers, and it's best to choose a simple recipe to start with.

- **6 lbs (2.8 kg) of Unhopped Pale Malt Extract** – Liquid malt comes in cans that are a little over 3 lbs each. Malt provides the sweet base that the yeast will feed on to make alcohol. Liquid malt extract is available from your local homebrew store. Dry malt extract is an acceptable alternative.

- **2.25 Oz (63 g) of East Kent Goldings Hops** – Hops add bitterness to your beer. Pellets are the most common and easy to store. Keep your unused hops in the freezer in airtight bags.
- **1 Package of Wyeast American Ale liquid Yeast (#1056)** or White Labs California Ale #WLP001. Liquid yeast makes very high quality beer, and is simpler to start with than dry yeast packets.
- **3.75 oz (106g) Priming Sugar** – such as corn sugar - also available from your brew store or grocer.

An Overview of the Brewing Process

Making beer at home consists of five stages:

- **Brewing the Beer** – Pale malt extract and hops are boiled together with water for about an hour to sterilize the extract and release the bittering qualities of the hops. Frequently grains are steeped in the mixture prior to the boil to add additional color and malt flavor complexity. Steeping will be covered in the next chapter.
- **Cooling and Fermenting** – The hot mixture (called wort) is cooled to room temperature and siphoned or transferred to a fermenter where it is combined with additional water to achieve the desired 5 gallon (19 l) batch size. Once the mixture drops to desired pitching temperature yeast is added to start the fermentation process. Cleanliness and sanitation are very important since bacteria in this state can easily infect the wort. An airlock is used to keep the fermenter sealed during fermentation. Your beer will ferment for 1-2 weeks.
- **Priming and Bottling** – Once the beer is fully fermented, it is siphoned to another container to prepare for bottling. Here priming sugars such as corn sugar are mixed with the

beer. The beer is siphoned into bottles and each bottle is capped with a bottle-capping device.

- **Aging** – Once the beer has been bottled it needs to age for 2-6 weeks. During aging the yeast will ferment the remaining sugar you added and create carbon dioxide. This carbon dioxide will naturally carbonate your beer so it is nice and bubbly. In addition, undesirable sediments such as excess yeast and proteins will drop out of the beer during aging and this will enhance the flavor of your beer. In may take several months to reach peak flavor, though homemade beer is usually drinkable after a month.

- **Drinking** – When the beer is properly aged – just put the bottles in the fridge and enjoy! There's nothing quite like a great beer that you made yourself.

This is the five step process for making your own beer. The brewing portion takes a few hours, and bottling and transferring take another few hours spread out over a few weeks. Overall, brewing a batch of extract beer involves 4-6 hours of your time and about 4 weeks to ferment and age into a drinkable brew. This makes home brewing an attractive hobby for people who lead a busy lifestyle.

Step 1 – Brewing
Brew day is my favorite part of the process. The smell of sweet wort bubbling away stirs something primeval in the human psyche. Since we are brewing an extract beer, there is not much preparation required for our first recipe.

You need a clean pot large enough to hold 2-3 gallons (12 l) of water plus the two cans (6+ lbs of extract) and boil it. I recommend a 4-5 gallon pot (19 l) or 7-9 gallons (34 l) if you plan to brew all-grain later. Put 2-3 gallons (11 l) of water into your pot and begin to heat it over your stove.

Once the water has heated up a bit, open your cans of extract and slowly mix them into the warm water. The malt extract will have the consistency of heavy syrup, and you may need some hot water to get it all out of the sides of the can. The combined water and extract mixture is called "wort" (pronounced as 'wert' which rhymes with Bert).

As you are adding the malt extract to your wort, you need to continuously mix it. If you do not mix it, the extract syrup will settle at the bottom of your pot where it will heat and caramelize, leaving a hardened caramel mess at the bottom of your pot. This carmelization can also alter the color and flavor of your beer, so it is important to mix well while heating.

Once you have all of your extract mixed in, the next step is to bring your wort to a boil. The water you used for your brew has a lot of air in it, and these small air bubbles will be released as it comes to a boil creating foaming and a high potential for a boil-over. One method to reduce foaming is to use a spray bottle filled with clean water to spray down the foam.

The best way to avoid a boil-over it to turn the heat down a bit as the wort just begins to boil, and then very carefully manage the heat during the first 15 minutes of the boil until you have a rolling boil with minimal foaming. Also, do NOT use a cover on your pot! While a covered pot will come to a boil quicker, the first time you open the pot it will boil over immediately – making a huge mess on your stove.

Once you achieve a steady boil it is time to add the hops. Weigh the proper amount and drop it in the hot wort. Some brewers use a mesh hops bag to reduce the mess later, but if you can cool your beer quickly most of the hops will drop out after the boil.

Stir occasionally during the boil to reduce the chance of extract settling to the bottom and caramelizing. I recommend you boil for 30-60 minutes. Boil time and size will affect your hop utilization and beer bitterness, so it is a good idea to use a tool like BeerSmith to balance your hops and boil time before you brew.

Step 2 – Cool and Ferment

When the boil has finished, you need to cool the hot wort to room temperature (72F/22C) as quickly as possible to reduce the chance of infection. Many beginning brewers immerse their pot in a cold ice bath. More advanced brewers will use a chiller such as an immersion coil that runs cold water through a coil of copper tubing to quickly cool the beer. If needed, add sterile water to the wort when you transfer it to your fermenter to achieve the target volume of 5 gallons.

The wort at this stage is very vulnerable to infection so you need to make sure that your fermenter; airlock, siphon tubes and anything else that touches the wort or yeast are thoroughly sanitized. I use a solution of 5 gallons (19 l) of water and small amount (1-2 oz or 30-60 ml) of household bleach to sanitize my equipment. However if you use bleach you must carefully rinse everything with hot water or you risk leaving your beer with a chlorine taste. Your brewing store also has no-rinse alternatives which we will cover shortly in the section on sanitation.

Your wort must be fully cooled to room temperature (72 F/22 C or less) and siphoned or dumped into your fermenter before you add (pitch) your yeast. The simplest method is to dump or siphon your wort into your fermenter, and then add some sterile cold water to the wort to rapidly cool it down. Be very careful when lifting your pot, as spilling hot wort on yourself could easily land you in the hospital. Don't worry about all of the junk (hops and proteins – called the "trub" in brewer's lingo) in the wort – most of it will fall to the bottom during fermentation.

Pitching yeast in hot wort will kill it, so wait until your wort has fully cooled to your fermentation temperature before adding yeast. I recommend the use of liquid yeast initially as it is easier to use than dry yeast. Liquid yeast comes in either a plastic tube or smack pack. The plastic tube type can be added directly to the wort. The foil smack-packs require you to pop an internal pouch containing the yeast several hours before pitching it to allow the yeast to grow in a self contained starter. Follow the instructions on the pouch to pop the internal pouch.

Carefully add the yeast to your fermenter. Once the yeast has been added and mixed in you may want to add some oxygen to the wort by splashing it around a bit. Then close the top, fit your airlock (which needs a little water in it) and set your beer in a dark cool place where the temperature is steady.

Your airlock should begin bubbling within 12-36 hours, and continue fermenting for about a week. If you see no bubbles from the airlock, check the fit on your plastic pail and airlock. Often plastic fermenters have a poor seal on the lid that leaks.

With a plastic fermenting barrel, you can check if the airlock has a poor seal by pressing gently on the lid and holding pressure for a few seconds. If there is a leak, the water level in the airlock will slowly return to its previous level. The bubbles in the airlock are CO_2 produced by the fermentation, and will slowly diminish as fermentation nears completion.

Assuming you have a good seal, the bubbles should slow to one every minute or two before you consider bottling. Don't open or break the seal on your fermenter airlock, as adding oxygen once the wort has started fermenting can harm your beer. Leave the beer alone, and let it ferment for 1-1/2 to 2 weeks before you bottle it.

Step 3 – Priming and Bottling

The final step before bottling your beer is called priming. Priming consists of mixing sugar in with the beer to carbonate the finished beer. The priming sugar will ferment in the bottle, creating a small amount of carbon dioxide, which will carbonate your beer.

Before you can prime and bottle, sanitize everything the beer will touch. Though your beer has fermented, it still can be ruined by bacteria or by adding too much oxygen to it (i.e. don't splash it around). Most brewers use a large plastic bucket or carboy to make it easy to mix the priming sugar evenly. Sterilize the bucket thoroughly, and also sterilize your siphoning equipment, tools and of course your bottles.

Make sure your bottles are clean and free of debris before sterilizing – use a bottle brush to remove any deposits. If you want to remove labels from reused bottles, soak them in a solution of ammonia and water overnight, then don some rubber gloves and rub the labels off. Do this in a well ventilated area, as ammonia fumes can be toxic. Also, never mix ammonia and bleach.

Sanitize bottles by soaking them in a weak bleach solution and then rinsing well, or use another sanitizing agent such as iodophor. I've also had some success with washing my bottles in the dishwasher, but you need to run it several times with no soap and hot water to avoid leaving a soap residue that will ruin the head retention on your beer.

Siphon the finished beer into your priming bucket, trying very hard not to splash it around or mix any air in with it. Add 3.75 oz (106 g) of priming sugar (I recommend corn sugar) to 5 gallons (19 l) of beer and very gently mix it in. Next siphon the beer into your bottles using your bottle filler. Be sure to leave at least an inch or more of empty space at the top of your bottle to aid in fermentation. Put the caps on each bottle as you go and later use your bottle capper to secure them.

Step 4 – Aging

The most difficult part of the brewing process is waiting for your beer to come of age. While beers are drinkable after a few weeks, the average homebrew reaches peak flavor anywhere from 8 weeks to 15 weeks after brewing. Most home brewers can't wait this long. During the aging process your beer will carbonate and excess yeast, tannins and proteins that create off flavors will fall out of your beer and settle to the bottom of the bottle. This will substantially improve your beer. I personally recommend waiting about 3-4 weeks after bottling before sampling your first brew.

Store your bottles in a cool, dark place. Unless you are brewing a lager under temperature controlled conditions, do not store your beer in the refrigerator for the first two weeks after bottling. Give it two weeks to fully carbonate at room temperature. After the first two weeks, refrigerating the beer will help it improve more quickly because the tannins, yeast and protein will sediment faster at cold temperature.

Step 5 – Drinking

The blessed day has finally arrived to sample your creation. During the aging process excess yeast, tannins and proteins will leave sediment at bottom of your bottle. Get a clean glass, open your brew, and gently poor most of your beer into the glass leaving only the sediment and a small amount of beer in your bottle. Don't worry if you take a little sediment into the glass – it won't hurt you. Smell the fresh beer, admire the frothy head, and then sip (don't guzzle) your first homebrew. Congratulations on your first beer!

Chapter 2: Extract Brewing Techniques

"The problem with the world is that
everyone is a few drinks behind" –
Humphrey Bogart

The first batch of beer is behind us, so now we're going to move forward to understand more about basic brewing ingredients, techniques, and processes. The first beer we brewed was an extract beer as we brewed it using the syrupy liquid barley malt extract. More advanced brewers make partial mash and all grain beers that use a technique called mashing to convert barley grain into wort. Before we jump into all grain brewing, we're going to learn more about malt extract brewing.

Brewing with Malt Extract

Brewing with malt extract (liquid or dry) is the starting point for most new brewers. Today many home brewers use malt extract as the dominant base for their beer. Brewing with extract offers some advantages over all-grain brewing. Less time and equipment is required.

While some purists point out that all-grain brewing gives you more control over certain ingredients in beer, the parade of award winning extract recipes in both local and national competition indicates that extract brewers are more than capable of going toe-to-toe with all grain brewers with regards to beer quality. To design a great beer recipe with malt extract it is important to understand its characteristics and limitations.

Malt extract is made by mashing grains using the same mashing process we will describe in later chapters to produce wort, a hot sweet sugary liquid. The wort is then concentrated from a thin liquid with original gravity of 1.080 to a thick syrup with gravity of between 1.400 and 1.450. The wort is concentrated by evaporation with added heat.

To reduce the heat required, the entire process is typically done under vacuum. Heating the wort to concentrate it also produces melanoidins, a color pigment that darkens the extract. This darkening process continues when boiling your extract. That is why wort made with even the palest malt extracts is significantly darker than corresponding all grain wort.

Liquid malt extract also contains water, an element that allows the coloring reaction to continue at a slow rate as the malt extract ages. Thus liquid malt extracts will continue to get darker as they age. Dry malt extract is not susceptible to this effect.

Beers made with malt extract will tend to ferment slower and finish at a higher gravity than corresponding all-grain beers. This is due to a variety of factors including the presence of unfermentable dextrins from the concentrating process and the lack of free nitrogen in extract malt needed for yeasts.   Also malt stored for an extended period tend to oxidize.

The last point worth mentioning, as both dry malt and liquid malt are prone to oxidizing when exposed to air or moisture for an extended period of time. All of these factors point to the critical importance of getting fresh malt extract whenever possible, and storing malt extracts in an airtight container in the refrigerator to minimize moisture and slow the effects of aging.

Tips for Brewing with Malt Extract
As long as proper care is taken in selecting and storing your extract, brewing with malt extract can be a real pleasure. To

enhance your malt extract recipes I recommend the following tips:

- Use pale malt extract as the base for your beer.
- To add color to your beer, steep dark grains (see the next section) rather than adding dark extract – this will enhance the body and flavor profile of your beer.
- Avoid using sugar in proportions larger than 10-20%. Some beginner kits instruct you to add large amounts of sugar. Sugar in large quantities can add off-flavors.
- For bitterness, boil with separate fresh hops (pellets, plugs or leaf). Many hop oils and bittering agents break down during storage in pre-hopped malt extracts. It's always better to go with fresh hops.
- Use steeped grains to enhance the color, body and flavor of your beer. From 2-5 pounds (0.91-2.27 kg) of steeped grains in a 5 gallon (19 l) batch will produce better beer than extract alone. Remember that some malts (munich, wheats, flaked and torrified malts) require mashing, and can't be steeped.
- As you boil malt extract, it will get darker. Consider using a late malt extract addition technique (covered later) if you are targeting a light to medium colored beer.
- If you are brewing a wheat beer, use wheat based extract. Similarly if brewing an Oktoberfest or Marzen beer use Munich based extract.
- Use a spreadsheet or brewing program such as BeerSmith at **BeerSmith.com** to estimate your color, bitterness and original gravity and match it against your target style. This will help you understand what each ingredient contributes to your beer.
- Be aware of the effect of the size of your boil pot on the bitterness of your beer. Small boil, high gravity malt extract batches will achieve significantly lower hops utilization than full size boils. Use a good spreadsheet or brewing program to estimate your bitterness before brewing.

- When converting an all-grain recipe to extract, take into account bitterness and color change as well as the base malt conversion. Extract recipes will generally need more hops and less colored additions than all-grain. Again, software can do much of the conversion for you more rapidly than you can manually.
- Use high attenuation yeasts with extract brews. Remember that extract beers generally ferment slower and leave a higher final gravity than expected.
- Store your malt extract in airtight containers, away from light sources, and ideally in a refrigerator to minimize oxidization and aging effects.

Malt extract brewers produce fantastic beer. Every year, even at the national level, malt extract brewers consistently finish in the winner's circle. I hope these tips will help you maximize the potential of malt extract brewing and helps you reach the winner's circle as well.

Steeping Grains

Steeped grains enhance the flavor and color of home brewed beer. Award winning extract beers all use some kind of steeped grains. Steeped grains add body, color, and fresh flavor to your homebrewed beer.

How to use Steeped Grains

Steeping grains is a remarkably simple method. The grains are added to 1.5 or 2 gallons (7.6 l) of plain water before the extracts are added. Heat plain water to between 150 and 170 degrees F (65-77 C), and then add the grains. The grains should be crushed to expose the sugars within the grain. It is usually best to put the grains in a grain bag from your local home brewing store to make them easy to remove, however, you can remove the grains by running the hot mixture through a strainer if necessary.

The grain bag will float at the top of the mixture. Leave it in the water and attempt to hold a constant temperature for 20-30 minutes. If you leave it in too long or steep at temperatures above 170F (77 C) you will extract excessive tannins, which will result in a dry astringent or band-aid flavor in the finished beer.

Steeped grains will not add many fermentables to your beer. Steeping grains, unlike mashing, does not convert the complex starches in the sugar into fermentable sugars, so only a small percentage of the steeped grain (< 10%) will ferment. However, since unfermentable proteins are added by steeping, the body and flavor of the beer will be increased.

Whenever possible, use freshly ground grains as crushed grains will slowly oxidize. If you leave your crushed grain exposed to air for more than a few weeks you may add off flavors to your beer. Storing your crushed grains in an airtight package in a refrigerator or freezer will help them to last longer, as hot temperature and moisture spoils the crushed grain more quickly.

Specialty grains are used for steeping. Caramel malt is often used to add body and color. Darker malts such as chocolate and black patent are also commonly used for flavor and color. Other popular additions include carafoam and carapils for body or roasted barley for a deep dark coffee flavor.

Not all grains are appropriate for steeping however. Pale malt, for example, adds very little flavor and should be mashed, not steeped. Flaked and torrified ingredients such as flaked barley, wheats, munich malt and oats also need to be mashed. To get a complete list of grains that may be mashed, visit our online grain listing (**beersmith.com/GrainList.htm**). Grains marked as "must mash" should, in general, be mashed and not steeped.

In order to properly use these ingredients, you need to switch to a partial mash or all-grain brewing method that will mash the ingredients to take full advantage of them.

Steeped grains add freshness and complexity to your extract beer, so try steeping some freshly crushed grains in your next batch of all extract beer.

Late Extract Additions

Using a late extract addition can improve the quality and color of your extract beer. Both liquid and dried malt extract beers suffer from an effect called carmelization when brewing. Carmelization occurs when liquid extract or excess sugars settle to the bottom of the brew pot during the boil and the sugars carmelize (harden) in the bottom of the pot.

This typically darkens the beer, and in extreme cases can also affect the taste of the beer. Obviously this is a problem for brewers of light colored beers. The effect is also common with high gravity beers in small brew pots because the boiling wort is thicker than with low gravity beer.

Adding Your Extract Late in the Boil

To avoid the ill effects of carmelization, malt extract brewers should delay the addition of the majority of their extracts until late in the boiling process. The extract must be added late enough in the boil to avoid carmelization, but early enough to assure that the extract is sterilized. Boiling the extract for about 15 minutes is a good balance.

I recommend adding a small amount of malt extract (perhaps 15-25%) early in the boil if using separate hops. The sugars and enzymes in the extract aid in extracting alpha acids (bitterness) from the hops. Boiling hops with a small amount of extract will result in smoother hop flavors and appropriate bitterness that you can't achieve with plain water alone.

Late extract additions do present one challenge for the brewer. Late extract additions will slightly increase the bitterness of the beer because they lower the boil gravity which increases hop utilization. The exact amount of bitterness added for late extracts can be complex to calculate, but programs like BeerSmith will do this for you. Another method is to calculate the hops addition without the late extract and then add 5-10% more hops to compensate for lower utilization during the last 15 minutes of the boil. We will cover how to calculate bitterness in a later chapter.

Cleaning and Sanitation

Sanitation is critical to brewing good beer at home. Even the slightest contamination of fermenting or finished beer can ruin a perfectly good batch. In this section, we take a look at good sanitation techniques for home brewers.

Good Brewing Sanitation

Anything that comes in contact with your wort or beer after it has been boiled should be both washed and sanitized. Items used prior to boiling should be washed, but need not be sanitized as boiling the wort will sanitize it.

Washing is simply the act of removing dust, dirt and grime from your equipment. Sanitizing your equipment is a separate step to kill off remaining bacteria and micro-organisms that might linger after washing. A thorough washing is a precursor to sanitizing, as sanitizing agents alone will not be able to remove built up grime and deposits on equipment that harbor bacteria.

Cleaning Agents

A mild anti-bacterial dish detergent makes a good primary cleaning agent. A scrubbing sponge or brush will help to remove any deposits, though be careful not to use abrasives on plastic as this tends to scratch and pit the plastic, creating a home for micro-organisms.

For stubborn stains, a number of stronger cleaning agents are available. These include Oxyclean, PBW, and Straight-A. Oxyclean is widely available in grocery stores, and as little as 1-3 tablespoons per 5 gallons (19 l) will rapidly clean the residue found on fermenter walls. Oxyclean is not compatible with aluminum pots, however. Powdered Brewing Wash (PBW) provides a somewhat stronger solution for tougher stains. Straight-A is another specialty cleaning agent that works well on tough stains. PBW and Straight-A are found in many home brewing specialty shops.

I use a mild detergent for day-to-day cleaning, and Oxyclean if I have a tough problem to clean up, as it is readily available at most retail stores and I clean my equipment right after using it. Note that all of the cleaning agents require a thorough rinse, as they all can leave a filmy deposit if not rinsed properly.

Do not leave bleach-based cleaners in contact with stainless steel for an extended period of time. A short wash is acceptable, but extended bleach exposure will pit stainless steel if left long enough. Similarly you should not soak plastic in cleaning agents for extended periods as plastic tends to absorb many of the chemicals.

Sanitizing Agents
After washing your equipment, it is important that anything that touches the wort or beer after boiling is thoroughly sanitized. Some of the most popular sterilizing agents include household bleach, iodophor, Star San and B-Brite.

Bleach is one of my favorite sanitizers as it is inexpensive and easy to get. Using 1 tbsp per gallon of water yields a solution that will sanitize with a soak time of 15 minutes. Some care needs to be taken when using bleach with stainless steel or plastics, as you should never exceed the 15 minute soak time. Rinse thoroughly with hot water.

Another sanitizer I use extensively is iodophor. Iodophor is an iodine-based sanitizer available in liquid form. I like to use iodophor for stainless pots and kegs as it works rapidly and it is not corrosive to steel like bleach. It requires a relatively small amount of iodophor (read the instructions – as concentrations vary) and will sanitize very quickly – as little as 60 seconds. Again you should not leave metals or plastics in contact for an extended period. Iodophor does not require rinsing, but I usually rinse lightly after use.

Star-san and B-Brite are available from your local homebrew store and are also easy to use. Star-san requires only 60 seconds to sanitize and does not require rinsing. B-Brite takes approximately 15 minutes to sanitize and does require mixing. B-Brite can also be used as a cleaning agent with a good soak. One advantage of star-san is that it can be stored for an extended period of time and reused several times.

Clean and sanitize any piece of equipment that comes in contact with your fermenting or fermented beer. This includes fermentation tubing, vessels, siphoning equipment, spoons, hydrometers, and your kegs or bottles. Clean, sanitary equipment will result in better beer that is free from infections.

Calibrating Your Brewing Equipment

Professional brewers will tell you that consistency is the the key to great beer. Most competitive home brewers are religious in their measurements and processes to ensure consistently great beer. However, many home brewers take their measurements at face value without bothering to calibrate them. This week we look at how to calibrate your equipment to make sure you have accurate measurements.

Hydrometers

A hydrometer is a simple floating device used to measure the specific gravity of your wort and finished beer. Accurate hydrometer readings are important for measuring your original gravity, understanding your brewhouse efficiency, and determining when fermentation is complete. Unfortunately some inexpensive brewing hydrometers are not very accurate.

The standard hydrometer is calibrated to read 1.000 when it is placed in distilled water at 60F (15.6 C). Some laboratory hydrometers are also calibrated to 68F (20 C), but these are rare. You can usually find the calibration temperature in small letters in the corner of the hydrometer scale.

To test your hydrometer, you need some distilled water in your sample tube or a vessel large enough to float the hydrometer. Place the water sample in your refrigerator until you reach the calibration temperature of 60F (15.6 C). Then immerse the hydrometer, shake any bubbles from the hydrometer surface and take the reading.

To read the hydometer properly, you should get your eye at the same level at the water, and find the bottom of the line where the air and water meet. If your hydrometer reads precisely 1.000, you have a calibrated hydrometer. Otherwise you will need to write down the value and subtract the difference from future readings. For example, if your hydrometer reads 1.002, you will need to subtract the difference (.002) from future readings when using this hydrometer.

Thermometers

Accurate thermometers are important, especially during the mashing process when temperatures are critical. Inexpensive brewing thermometers can be off by several degrees. Fortunately thermometers are also easy to calibrate, using the same distilled water you had for your hydrometer calibration.

Start by freezing some distilled water in a cup. Then break up the ice into chunks and immerse it in some distilled water. Let it sit for at least 8-10 minutes to reach equilibrium and then drop the thermometer in and read the temperature. If your thermometer is at 32 F (0 C), you have a properly calibrated thermometer. If it is high or low, you will again need to make an adjustment by that amount every time you use the thermometer.

Vessels

Knowing at a glance the volume of your vessels (boil pots, fermenters, mash tuns) makes brewing much easier and more accurate. If your vessel does not have volume marks on it, you can add your own by using a smaller measuring vessel to accurately measure volumes. You can start with a large measuring cup or gradated water bottle to measure quarts or liters. If you don't have a quart/liter size measure, start with a small measuring cup and disposable 2 liter soda bottle and make your own quart or liter measure by filling the bottle using the measuring cup and marking the outside of it with a permanent marker.

Once you have your quart or liter measure, you can fill your larger fermenter or boil pot slowly and accurately to create your measuring marks. For a plastic vessel, mark the outside of it using a permanent pen. For a metal vessel you can score or etch it. If you don't have an easy way to mark the vessel, you can create a dip stick from a small dowel and mark volumes with notches on it. Some brewers even notch their large brewing spoon to track volume.

Consistency is critical for great beer, and calibrated equipment leads to consistency, so take a few minutes to calibrate your equipment up front.

Yeast and Fermentation

Yeast, in particular, has improved dramatically in the last 20 years. When I started, the only yeast available was dry packet "bread-style" yeast. It came in two flavors – ale and lager. The quality of these two yeast strains was questionable, resulting in significant variation in flavor and character.

In the early 1990's Wyeast and White Labs introduced high quality liquid yeasts to the US homebrewing market. Companies like SafAle also brought high quality dry yeasts into the picture. This revolutionized homebrewing in a way that is difficult to explain today.

Brewing Yeast

Brewing yeast is a single cell microorganism (technically a fungi), and both ale and lager yeasts are members of the family Saccharymyces Cerevisiae. Lager yeast was earlier classified as S. Uvarum, but a recent reclassification put it in the S. Cerevisiae family. Ales are traditionally called "top fermenting" for the yeast layer that forms at the top of the fermenter, while lagers are called "bottom fermenting."

Ale yeasts ferment in the temperature range 50-77F (10-25C) and produce beers higher in esters and often lower in attenuation (in next section), both distinctive characteristics of ales. Esters add a fruity, banana like complexity to your beer. Ale yeast strains are often mixed together to aid in attenuation and flocculation (see next section). Lagers ferment in the range from 44-59F (7-15C) and produce a cleaner beer with lower esters.

The Fermentation Life Cycle

Yeast goes through four overlapping phases when fermenting beer into wort. After pitching, yeast starts in the "Lag Phase". During the lag phase, the yeast strives to reproduce as fast as possible. The key ingredient during this phase is Glycogen, a sugar stored internally in the yeast, which is broken into glucose to fuel yeast reproduction. If an insufficient amount of yeast is pitched (or the yeast itself is low in glycogen), you will get an excess of diacetyl (buttery or butterscotch flavor) in your finished beer. A properly sized yeast starter is critical, and we will show you how to calculate the size of your yeast starter shortly.

The lag phase is followed quickly by the respiration (also called the growth) phase. In the growth phase, yeast cells grow logarithmically (usually one to three doublings) by cellular division. In this phase the critical ingredients are oxygen and a variety of yeast nutrients. The cells will continue to grow until the oxygen or nutrients have been depleted.

Once all of the oxygen has been scrubbed from the wort, the fermentation phase begins. Yeast cells convert simple sugars into carbon dioxide, alcohol and beer flavors. As the sugars are consumed, the gravity of the beer will rapidly drop. Fermentation normally takes 3-7 days.

Sedimentation is the final phase of fermentation. Yeast will begin to form into clumps and settle to the bottom of the fermenter in a process called flocculation. In this phase, yeast will also store the glycogen needed for future reproduction as it prepares to enter a dormant state. Some yeast will settle (flocculate) much more rapidly than others, so settling can take from days to weeks depending on the yeast variety.

Understanding Yeast Characteristics

Selecting a yeast appropriate for a given beer involves some knowledge of key yeast characteristics:

- **Attenuation**: Refers to the percentage of sugars converted to alcohol and CO2. A high attenuation yeast will result in a clean, dry finish. Low attenuation yeasts typically leave ester, malt and other flavors behind for a more full bodied complex beer flavor.

- **Flocculation**: Flocculation refers to the ability of yeast to form clumps (flocs) at the end of fermentation and rapidly sediment (or be skimmed) from the finished beer. Low flocculation yeast is often called "powdery" yeast. High flocculation yeasts tend to fall out of the beer before completing fermentation, leaving a more complex, higher gravity beer. Low flocculation yeasts such as lagers will completely ferment, leaving a cleaner finish, but it can then be difficult to separate the yeast from the beer.

- **Temperature Range**: Different yeast strains have differing temperature tolerances. Ales ferment at a warmer temperature than lager. Higher temperature fermentation for ales is associated with higher ester production, and lower temperature lagers with clean dry flavors.

- **Alcohol Tolerance**: Many types of yeast are sensitive to alcohol content, and will have trouble fermenting very high original gravity wort. Champagne, Wine, or other alcohol tolerant yeasts are frequently used either for primary fermentation or as a second yeast addition to assure full fermentation of very high gravity beers such as barley wine.

- **Beer Flavor**: Individual yeast strains can add widely varying flavor profiles to your beer. A good example is Hefe-Weizen, where a significant majority of the clove and banana beer flavor comes directly from the yeast. Matching the yeast strain to the style of beer is one way to provide proper flavor balance.

An Example of Yeast in Beer Design

In most cases, brewers tend to select the Wyeast or White Labs yeast that matches their beer style. Let's look at one example where varying from the script might pay off. One example is brewing an Irish Stout. Irish stout has a very dry roasted character derived from roasted barley.

A traditional yeast choice might be an Irish Ale yeast such as White labs WLP004. However, looking at WLP004, it has a modest attenuation of 71.5%, which will produce a more fruity finish. One could experiment by picking WLP007, "Dry English Ale" yeast. This yeast has a much higher attenuation (75%) and will leave a drier finish on the beer, while still retaining some of the English esters needed for the stout.

At the other extreme, I know several brewers that use a single strain, White Labs California Ale WLP001 for just about every beer they brew. Their justification is that this yeast is relatively flavor neutral for an ale yeast, has a very high attenuation and leaves a clean finish on any beer. It ferments rapidly and flocculates quickly from the beer minimizing storage time needed. Personally, I don't subscribe to this "one size fits all" approach, but a number of brewers have demonstrated great success with it.

The above are just examples, but the key to great beer design is to understand the ingredients you are working with. Knowledge of the characteristics of yeast, and its significant effect on your beer will help you to become a better brewer.

Using a Yeast Starter

The quality of your homebrew can be dramatically improved by making a yeast starter. Home brewers often toss a packet or vial of yeast into their beer without much thought to the quantity needed. Though modern liquid brewer's yeast smack packs and vials are a huge improvement over older dry yeast packs, these packages do not contain enough yeast cells for optimal fermentation results. Underpitching results in slower startup, higher risk of infection, off-flavors and sometimes incomplete fermentation. Adding too much yeast is also bad as it can lead to incomplete fermentation cycles.

How Much Yeast is Enough?

In general, lagers require a larger starter than ales. George Fix's book "An Analysis of Brewing Techniques" recommends pitching rates of 0.75 million cells for ales and 1.5 million cells for lagers. The number is measures in million of cells per milliliter per degree Plato.

Converting to homebrew units, his ale figure translates to 4 billion cells per point of original gravity per 5 gallon (19 l) batch. A 5 gallon sample beer with 1.048 original gravity would provide 48 points which is 4 billion cells/pt x 48 points = 192 billion cells. So 192 billion cells are required for this batch.

An average White Labs yeast vial contains around 100 billion cells of active yeast. Therefore without a starter, you would need two yeast vials to reach optimal pitching for our 5 gallon (19 l) example. The large Wyeast activator packs contain around 100 billion cells as well, so again you would need two packs. The smaller smack packs contain only 15-18 billion active cells, so you would need 11 packs for the same 5 gallon (19 l) batch. Keep in mind you would need to double the above figures for a lager.

Fortunately, creating a starter is an excellent alternative to purchasing large quantities of yeast. Research varies, but a starter of 1 quart (or liter) will yield approx 150 billion cells and a two quart (or liter) starter will yield from 200-240 billion cells. So a 1.5-2 quart/liter starter is sufficient for an average 5 gallon (19 l) ale. For a 10 gallon batch, a 4 quart/liter starter is appropriate (up to 400 billion cells yielded) but may require a two step starter (first a 1 quart/liter starter, then transfer it to a 4 quart/liter starter) if you are pitching less than 100 billion cells initially. For a lager we need to roughly double these sizes.

Making the Starter

Creating a starter is very easy. You want to start 18-24 hours before your brewing session, so the yeast can reach an active state before pitching. If you are doing a two stage starter, allow 18-24 hours for each stage. I use a large Pyrex flask, but a very clean pot is a suitable substitute if you can cool it quickly. Dry malt extract is easy to store and use in small quantities. To determine the amount to add, you can create a mini-recipe in BeerSmith that is the size of your starter and adjust for a target gravity of around 1.040. Alternately, use this rule of thumb: between 3.5 and 4 ounces (100-113 g) of dry extract per quart (or liter) will give you a good starter.

Dissolve the dry malt extract, boil it for 10-15 minutes to make sure it is sterile, and then cool it quickly in an ice bath and transfer it to a sanitized container. Once it reaches room temperature, pitch your yeast and seal the container with an airlock to prevent contamination.

Allow the starter to ferment between 18 and 24 hours before you brew. Pitch the entire contents of the starter into your batch of beer to get an active, robust start. Pitching yeast at the proper rate will significantly reduce the lag before active fermentation begins, promote complete fermentation, reduce the risk of infection and improve the overall quality of your beer.

Chilling your Wort

When brewing beer, it's critical to quickly cool your brew before adding yeast to minimize the chance of infection. In this section, we look at the advantages of rapidly cooling your wort after boiling, and also how to build a simple immersion chiller using copper tubing purchased from your local hardware store.

Some of the advantages include:

- **Reducing the chance of infection** – Your wort is vulnerable to bacterial infection when it is warm and has no yeast added. You want to minimize the chance of infection by cooling rapidly and pitching the yeast as soon as practical.
- **Improved clarity** – When you rapidly cool hot wort, many of the heavy proteins and tannins will no longer be soluble and will fall out of the wort. Siphoning the wort off of this "cold break" will result in an improved clarity and improve taste as well.
- **Reduction of volatile compounds** – Dimethyl Sulfide (DMS) which gives beer a strong "sweet corn" flavor can continue to break down after boiling and may be carried forward into the finished beer unless you rapidly cool the beer.

Quickly cooling 5-10 gallons (10-19 l) of boiling hot wort does present some problems for the home brewer. Ideally you would like to reach fermentation temperature as quickly as possible, though something in the 10-20 minute range is acceptable. Commercial brewers use elaborate two-stage heat exchangers with a glycol coolant to achieve the final fermentation temperature.

Home brewers often choose something a bit less elaborate. Some popular wort cooling systems include:

Ice Bath
Often beginners immerse their entire boiling pot into a tub full of ice water, or you can add chilled water as I recommended in chapter one. This can be an effective method, but it typically takes longer than the methods listed below, since heat can only be transferred through the hot pot itself.

Immersion Chillers

A popular solution with home brewers, the immersion chiller is a coil of 30-50 feet of copper tubing that is immersed in the hot wort in the pot. The tubing is connected to a sink or garden hose and cool water is continuously run through the chiller to cool the wort. Since 50 feet of copper tubing has a large surface area, 5-10 gallons of wort can be chilled rapidly using this method.

Immersion chillers may also include a second stage, consisting of an additional coil before the main coil that is immersed in an ice water bath to lower the temperature of the water as it goes into the wort. A two stage immersion chiller cools even more quickly and helps in cases where the tap water going into the chiller might be at or near the desired fermentation temperature.

Immersion chillers are also very easy to make, as described below, and also easy to clean since the outside of the coil simply needs to be wiped down and washed after use.

Counter-flow Chillers

A counter-flow chiller is a coil that contains two tubes of different diameters, one placed inside of the other. Cold water is pumped through the outer tube while the wort is siphoned or pumped in the opposite direction in the inner tube. Counter-flow chillers are extremely efficient and can cool wort very quickly.

The only downside for home brewers is that they can be more difficult to clean and sterilize. As soon as you finish using a counter-flow chiller, you need to flush it rapidly with hot water and run cleaning fluid through it. Also it is a bit harder to construct a counter-flow chiller at home.

Building an Immersion Chiller

An immersion chiller is simple for the average brewer to construct and maintain. The basic materials can be bought at the local hardware store and assembled in about 30 minutes.

Materials Needed:

- 50 feet of 3/8" outer diameter copper tubing
- 20 feet of 3/8" inner diameter plastic tubing
- 4-6 3/8" hose clamps
- Garden hose adapter (female)
- Compression fittings/adapters to mate garden hose adapter to the 3/8" copper tubing

Start by making a large diameter coil from the copper tubing. Make the coil small enough to fit in your boil pot. The best way to form the coil is to wrap the tubing around a large coffee can, bottom of a corney keg, or other large cylinder.

Leave both ends of the copper tubing sticking up above the height of your pot, and bend them 90 degrees so they extend horizontally over the edges. On one end, attach the fittings to the garden hose adapter, and to the other attach your plastic hose with clamps. Attach the garden hose and run water through it to check for leaks.

For a two stage cooler, attach a second smaller coil to one end and place the garden hose fitting on it. Join the two coils with a length of plastic tubing. When operating, place the first coil into a cold bath of ice water and the second into your wort. This will cool the water going into the wort, making your system more efficient.

Aeration for Home Brewing

Aeration with oxygen is very important for optimal fermentation of beer, but needs to be applied at the right time to brew good beer. Let's take a look at aeration and how it can help you brew great beer at home.

Aeration Explained

Let's start with some basic definitions. Aeration is the injection of oxygen into the wort during the brewing process, usually after boiling and cooling and just prior to fermentation. The act of boiling wort forces most of the oxygen out of the wort. Unfortunately, as we covered in the earlier section on fermentation and the yeast life cycle, yeast requires a great deal of oxygen during the "lag phase" when it is rapidly multiplying in the wort. Without enough oxygen, the yeast will fail to reproduce sufficiently, leaving an incomplete fermentation.

Before we get to how to best add more oxygen, let's look at two other important terms. Another term you may hear is "hot side aeration", which refers to excessive splashing or aeration of the wort during the boil or before we've had a chance to cool the wort down. The problem with adding oxygen while the wort is hot is that it can oxidize the melanoidins in your beer leading to a stale flavor. A study by George Fix suggests that hot side aeration can occur at temperatures as low as 86F (30 C) (which is pretty low!), so it is important to cool your wort before aerating it.

A third term, called oxidation, is closely related to the first two. Oxidation occurs when you add oxygen after the lag phase of yeast growth (i.e. later in fermentation, or after the beer has fermented). In this case, the effect is exactly what is seen when you left your pony keg at college out for a few days with an air pump on it. The air oxidizes the finished beer, leaving a strong stale flavor. So, you clearly don't want to introduce oxygen in your beer after lag fermentation has started.

Aerating your Wort

So far we've learned that hot side aeration is bad, oxidation is bad, but proper aeration of the cooled wort is good. Now let's look at how to put this information to good use in our beer. Yeast needs between 8 and 10 parts per million (ppm) of oxygen to properly reproduce in the lag phase. A level of 8ppm is achievable using air alone (which is 21% oxygen), but achieving a higher level requires a tank of pure oxygen.

The best time to aerate your wort is as soon as it is cool. Ideally this can be done during transfer to the fermenter or immediately after transfer to the fermenter. If you aerate after pitching your wort, do not aerate for long as the lag phase generally starts within a few hours of pitching the wort.

There are three basic methods for aerating wort:

- **Splashing** – Splashing the wort around in the fermenter can actually add some oxygen to the solution. You can achieve this by splashing the wort around during transfer – for example using a cap at the end of the siphon that splashes the wort out the side a bit. While splashing will not achieve as high as oxygen content as injection, it is a good option for those on a limited budget. Splashing is far superior to no aeration at all.
- **Agitation** – Agitation is done by stirring rapidly with a spoon, whisking the wort around with a whisk or rocking the entire fermenter. A sterilized whisk is best if you have open access to the wort. Whisk the wort vigorously for several minutes before adding your yeast. Agitation is a step above splashing, as it generally gets more oxygen into the solution.
- **Injection** – There are many ways to inject air or oxygen directly into the wort. The simplest setup involves using an inexpensive aquarium pump with an inline sterile filter. Note that the filter is needed to prevent bacteria and other organisms from being drawn in with the air. I also

recommend using some kind of carbonation stone or aeration stone at the end of the tube to help diffuse the air. Care must be taken to sanitize the stone and tube before using it. A more elaborate injection system would use an actual oxygen bottle and regulator to inject oxygen. However, even the relatively cheap aquarium pump injection system can achieve the 8 ppm ideal aeration level needed for your wort.

For many years, I used the splashing/agitation system, but for less than $25 you can move up to an aquarium pump, filter and carbonation stone and significantly improve the fermentation of your beer.

Bottling Tips

Bottling beer can be tedious, which is why many brewers eventually make the switch to kegging. Home brewers say that bottling is their least favorite part of the brewing process. To help ease the pain, here are 10 tips on bottling your home brewed beer.

- **Inspect your Bottles Before Use** – Inspect each bottle by holding it up in front of a window or light source and looking straight down the bottle. Bottles tend to chip and crack either around the mouth or bottom of the bottle, and they also tend to collect mold and other debris at the very bottom. Discard bad bottles to avoid a potential bottle bomb. Choose well made heavier bottles if possible and never use twist off bottles!
- **Remove Labels with Ammonia** – Soak recycled bottles overnight in a solution of water and ammonia. After soaking, you will be able to gently rub off most bottle labels with your hands. Be sure to wear rubber gloves and work in a well ventilated area, as the ammonia gas can be dangerous.

- **Use a "Jet Bottle Washer" and Bottle Brush** - Used bottles frequently have clumps of mold in the bottom that can be difficult to remove. A "Jet Bottle Washer" washer is a device that screws onto the end of your faucet and has a valve on it that activates when you push the bottle over it. A bottle jet will make short work of cleaning most bottles. For stubborn sediment, a small bottle brush will remove the rest. Sanitize your bottles in a high quality sanitizing solution before bottling.

- **Don't Bottle Directly from the Fermenter** – Siphon your beer off the fermenter and into a temporary priming bucket or carboy when bottling. Minimize splashing, as air can easily oxidize your finished beer. Mix your priming sugar in while the beer is still in your priming bucket. This will help reduce the amount of sediment in your finished bottles, and also assure that the priming sugar is evenly mixed into your beer.

- **Use Fining Agents a Few Days Before Bottling** – Fining agents help to clarify your beer and reduce sediment in the finished bottles, but they need to be added well before bottling. Additions such as gelatin and polyclar should be added after active fermentation, but 5-7 days before bottling to give them time to settle as much of the excess yeast and proteins from the finished beer as possible. (Fining agents are covered in detail in chapter 8).

- **Weigh your Priming Sugar** - Avoid the habit of just adding 3/4 cup (177 ml) of corn sugar to your beer. Sugars vary widely in density, so one cup of a corn sugar may not be the same as another. Calculate the weight of the priming sugar needed for your target carbonation level using a tool such as BeerSmith or an online calculator and then weigh the sugar or DME before adding it.

- **Purchase a Good Bottle Capper** – If you have ever used a cheap bottle capper, then you understand how important this piece of advice is. There are many different styles of bottle cappers, and all can work well, but spend a few extra dollars on a well made capper. Ask your local homebrew storeowner which one he recommends. The extra dollars will save you the pain of broken bottles on bottling day.

- **Oxygen Absorbing Bottle Caps or Not?** – Oxygen absorbing bottle caps are a popular item, but are they really needed? Unless you are planning to store your beer for an extended period (a year or more), the answer is no. The oxygen in the headspace of the bottle during bottling is consumed in part by fermentation of the priming sugar. In addition, CO2 is produced during fermentation of the priming sugar that helps protect the beer. As long as the caps are tight and properly sealed, there should be little risk of oxidization.

- **Fill bottles to the Brim** – Bottles need the correct amount of headspace (air) at the top of the bottle for carbonation and proper pressure. If you are using a wand type of bottle filler, you can generally fill your bottles very close to the top before removing the wand. This should leave about 1″ to 1-1/2″ (2.5-3.8 cm) of headspace in the neck of the bottle, which will work well for carbonating your beer.

- **Store your Bottles Properly** – After capping the bottles, store them at fermentation temperature for at least two weeks to allow proper fermentation of the priming sugar for carbonation. After that, store your beer in a cool place away from light. If you want to clear the beer more quickly, consider lagering (cold storing) your beer in the refrigerator. After use, rinse your bottles clean and store them upside down to make it easy to clean them next time.

Chapter 3: Beer Recipe Design

*"Give a man a fish and he will eat for a
day. Teach him how to fish, and he will sit
in a boat and drink beer all day." -*
Anonymous

After you have a few batches of beer under your belt, you will
want to understand the basics of recipe design. Recipe design
is an important topic both for creating your own recipes, and
adjusting recipes from a book or the web to fit your own
brewing style and equipment.

Recipe Design Fundamentals

Over the years, I've come to realize that even experienced
brewers misunderstand the basic principles of beer recipes
design. In this chapter we're going to introduce some methods
to design some great beer recipes at home. What follows is an
overview of what I consider the essence of beer recipe design.

Starting a New Recipe

When I build a new beer recipe, I almost always start by
picking a target beer style. This is not to say that the style
defines the whole beer as there is plenty of room for
interpretation and creativity, but by starting with a beer style,
you establish the baseline for the beer you are going to brew.

A good starting reference is the Beer Judge Certification
Program (BJCP) style guidelines (from the web site **bjcp.org**).
This beer style guideline provides detailed specifications and
suggested ingredients for nearly 100 different styles of beer.
These guidelines also provide ranges for typical bitterness,
color and original gravity for the beer that can help you achieve
the appropriate balance for the beer.

Choosing the Ingredients

The next step in designing the beer is to pick appropriate ingredients. Beer is made from malt, hops, water and yeast (occasionally with a few spices). Before you jump to doing detailed design, do a bit of research to determine what ingredients in each category are typically used your target beer style, and in roughly what proportions. For proportions, I prefer to work initially in percentages such as 80% pale malt, 15% caramel malt and 5% chocolate malt – this makes it easier to scale things later on.

The BJCP style guide provides some information on typical ingredients used, but often does not have detailed breakouts of proportions. The style articles in the latter half of this book do provide more detailed information on the history of different beer styles and percentage of ingredients used. A number of online beer recipe sites have some great examples, though one must be careful when using someone else's recipe as often they are far from the traditional or historical beer style.

Another great resource is brewing books – one of my favorites is Ray Daniel's book <u>Designing Great Beers</u>, which has detailed analysis of percentages of ingredients used in award winning and commercial beer examples for many styles. Finally, you can often find articles or messages for a particular beer style using a simple web search or search on an online discussion forum.

The goal of all of your research is to determine ingredients appropriate to the style. Using the wrong ingredients, or selecting the wrong proportions will result in a beer with the wrong flavor and balance. For example, an English Bitter with American citrus hops would be atypical and likely deemed outside of the traditional style. You will rarely go wrong using ingredients that are authentic to the style.

Brewing by the Numbers

Once you have your ingredients selected, and have them apportioned in roughly the correct way it's time to actually enter the beer into a spreadsheet or program such as BeerSmith from **BeerSmith.com**, and run the numbers. This is an important step, which many beginning brewers skip, but if you don't have the recipe properly adjusted and balanced for your equipment and your settings you will likely end up way off your target style.

The critical parameters to look at as you enter and adjust your ingredients include the following. We're going to cover many of these in additional detail later in this chapter.

- **Original Gravity (OG)–** A measure of how much fermentable and unfermentable malt you have added to the beer. You measure the original gravity of your unfermented wort using a hydrometer after you transfer the beer into your fermenter. The original gravity typically determines how much potential alcohol you will have in the beer, as well as how malty the beer will be. The style guideline provides a range for this parameter.
- **Bitterness (IBUs)** – Bitterness from hops balances the flavor of your beer. For beer design, you want to estimate your bitterness in International Bitterness Units (IBUs). We will cover calculation of IBUs later in this chapter. Again you want to use the style guideline to determine the appropriate IBU range.
- **Color (SRM)** – You can estimate the color of your beer from the ingredients using a calculation we will cover shortly. Estimating the color is important, as you don't want your pale ale to be black or your stout to be blonde in color. Obviously darker malts add color.
- **Bitterness Ratio (IBU/GU)** – The bitterness ratio gives you a rough measurement of the bitterness to malt balance for the beer. A hoppy beer will have a high bitterness ratio,

while a malty beer will have a low one. We will show you how to calculate the bitterness ratio shortly as well.

- **Final Gravity (FG)** – Final gravity is measured with a hydrometer after fermentation is complete. While it is very difficult to accurately predict final gravity ahead of time, I often look at the final gravity for the style to get an idea of the attenuation needed from the yeast. Some styles require high attenuation yeast to achieve a smooth clean flavor, while others need low attenuation yeasts for complex flavor.

- **Carbonation** – The carbonation of the beer should match the style. Carbonation is measured in volumes (vols), where one volume would essentially be a liter of carbon dioxide gas dissolved into a liter of beer. Fermented beer at room temperature with no additional carbonation contains about 1.0 volumes of CO_2. Authentic English ales are often served with little or no carbonation (1.5-2.0 vols) while many German beers are highly carbonated (up to 3.0 vols). If you research the style, you can often determine the correct carbonation level for the beer.

Brewing Techniques

After you have the proper ingredients and have balanced the recipe by the numbers, the final step is to look at the techniques needed to brew this style of beer. Different styles definitely require application of a variety of brewing techniques. Some of the techniques we will cover in the coming chapters include:

- **Hop Techniques** – A variety of hop techniques are available, most of which are covered in the upcoming chapter on hops. Examples include first wort hopping, dry hopping, late hop additions, bittering hops, and use of a hopback. Different beer styles require different methods to achieve the appropriate balance.

- **Mash Techniques** – For all grain and partial mash brewers, adjusting your mash temperature is critical to achieving the appropriate body for your beer. Lower mash temperature during the main conversion step will result in a lower body beer and higher mash temperatures result in more body. In addition, advanced brewers may want to consider techniques like decoction mashing or a multi-step mash if appropriate to the style.

- **Fermenting, Lagering and Aging** – The temperature for fermenting your beer should be appropriate for the yeast and beer you are using. Yeast manufacturers listings as well as most brewing software include appropriate temperature ranges for fermentation of each type of yeast strain. Aging and lagering should also match your target style.

Beer design is clearly one part art, and one part science, which is what makes it an interesting and enjoyable hobby. However, if you do your homework, select quality ingredients, run the numbers and follow good brewing techniques you can make fantastic beer at home using your own recipes.

Understanding Beer Color

Beer spans an endless array of colors. The deep black color and white foam of an Irish Stout, deep copper of a Pale Ale and cloudy light color of a Bavarian Wheat are all within the rainbow we call beer. In this section, we'll look at beer color, how it's measured, color limitations, and how to estimate the color of a beer recipe.

The History of Beer Color

The system used to characterize beer color has its origins in the late 1800's. The original lovibond system was created by J.W. Lovibond in 1883, and used colored slides that were compared to the beer color to determine approximate value. For decades, beer was compared to colored glass standards to determine the Lovibond color, and we still use the term "Degrees Lovibond" extensively today to describe the color of grains.

Over time, limitations of the Lovibond were recognized, not the least of which was that it depended upon a person's vision – which naturally has variations in color perception from person to person. By the mid-20'th century, light spectrophotometer technology was developed. In 1950 the ASBC adopted the Standard Reference Method (SRM) color system. Separately the Europeans developed another visual system called the European Brewing Convention (EBC). It originally used visual comparison, but some 25 years later changed to use a spectrophotometer in a slightly different way than SRM.

Measuring Beer Color

The SRM color of beer is measured using a ½" glass cuvette measured by a spectrophotometer at a light wavelength of 430nm. The SRM color is approximately 10 times the amount of absorbance, which is measured on a logarithmic scale. The SRM color is approximately equal to the old lovibond scale in most cases. The other common method, called the European Brewing Convention (EBC) is measured at the same wavelength but in a smaller 1 cm cuvette. In practice the EBC color is approximately 1.97 times the SRM color. (EBC = 1.97 * SRM).

If you don't have a spectrophotometer handy in your personal laboratory, a number of tools are available to help you measure the color of your beer. The most popular and easy to use is a beer reference color card, such as the Davidson guide, to do a visual comparison of your beer against standard reference colors. I recommend purchasing such a guide or color card from your local store. I don't recommend printing an online color card, as the variations in printer color will spoil your measurements.

Another method involves diluting your beer with distilled water and comparing it to known color standards such as mass produced commercial beer. Ray Daniels describes using commercial beer references in detail in his chapter on beer color from his book Designing Great Beers.

Estimating Beer Color for a Recipe

As a home brewer, I'm very interested in how to estimate the color of my beer for a given recipe in advance of brewing. In practice, good home brewing software like BeerSmith will automatically estimate the color of your recipe as you build it, but I think it is still useful to know what is going on under the hood.

A first iteration at estimating beer color involved simply calculating the Malt Color Units (MCUs) of a recipe.

MCU = (Weight_grain_in_lbs) * (Color_of_grain_in degrees_lovibond) / (volume_in_gallons)

For multiple grain additions, you can simply calculate the MCU for each addition and add them together. MCU provides a good estimate of SRM color for light beers, but starts to diverge as beer color exceeds 6-8 SRM, because light absorbance is logarithmic and not linear. For a more accurate estimate that holds for darker beers up to about 50 SRM, we turn to the Morey equation:

SRM color = 1.4922 * (MCU ** 0.6859)

The Morey equation provides an excellent estimate of beer color throughout the range from 1-50 SRM, and is the one used by most brewers today.

Limitations of Beer Color and Color Estimates

No matter how accurately your color estimate or measurement is, you need to recognize that all existing beer color systems have very real limitations. The SRM color system, for instance, is measured from the absorbance of a single wavelength of light. It can't tell the difference between similarly colored red beers and amber beer, for example. The subtle hues of red and brown may look identical at the 430nm wavelength.

In fact, it is not possible to specify the precise color of a beer with a single "beer darkness number" such as SRM. The subtle variations in red, brown, gold, copper and straw can't be captured in a single dimension beer color system. Irish Red is a good example – if you do an estimate of the color for an Irish Red you will likely get something that does not look very red at all on the color card. Yet, the addition of a tiny amount of roasted barley gives it the distinctive red hue that the SRM system simply can't capture.

Extract brewers need to be aware that liquid extracts in particular tend to get darker as they age, and also that extracts will darken in a process called carmelization as they boil. Both the aging of extracts and carmelization were covered in chapter 2. The net result of the aging and boiling effect is that many extract beers come out substantially darker than an estimate would indicate.

In practice, these issues are not a problem for the average home brewer, but commercial breweries often use coloring agents, mixing of batches and other techniques to achieve very precise color matching from batch to batch. For a home brewer, it is enough to know that a color estimate has limitations.

Hop Bitterness

How much beer hops is enough? It is important to understand the quantity of hops you need to properly balance your home brewed beer. Hops are a precious and often expensive commodity. Knowing exactly how much to use for your target equipment and beer style can save you a lot of money and enhance the quality of your finished beer.

Home Bitterness Units

My first book as a homebrewer was Charles Papazian's excellent work The Complete Joy of Homebrewing. In his book he introduces the Home Bitterness Unit (HBU) defined simply as the number of ounces of hops times the alpha content for that hops. Fuggles hops have an alpha acid content of about 4.5%, so 2 ounces of Fuggles hops would be 9 HBUs.

While HBUs are easy to calculate for beginners, they are not very accurate. An accurate estimate of bitterness depends on important factors like the size of the batch, size of the boil, original gravity, and boil time for the hops. HBUs just don't do it!

A much more accurate method to determine beer bitterness is the International Bitterness Unit (IBU). An IBU is measured directly using a formula with a spectrophotometer and solvent extraction. Professionals and advanced brewers use IBUs estimates exclusively to help them design world class beers.

Beer Style guides such as the BJCP Style Guide (**bjcp.org**) list the bitterness range in IBUs for dozens of beer styles. This provides an excellent guide for anyone who wants to know how much hops to add for a particular beer style. You can adjust your bitterness in IBUs to be within the beer style range.

Estimating IBUs

Measuring the actual IBU content of a beer requires a laboratory. As a practical substitute for an elaborate lab, home brewers use equations to estimate the IBU content of their beer. A simplified equation from Ray Daniel's Book Designing Great Beers for IBUs is:

$$IBUs = U\% * (ALPHA\% * W\_OZ * 7489) / (V\_GAL)$$

Where U% is the hop utilization in percent, ALPHA% is the percent alpha for the hop variety, W_OZ is the hop weight in ounces, and V_GAL is the volume of hops in gallons. This gives the IBUs for a single hop addition. If you have multiple hop additions, you need to add up the IBUs from each.

In this equation, the utilization percentage (U%) is the one factor that varies depending on equipment used, brewing methods used, boil time, boil size, and boil gravity. The variations between different hop estimation equations basically come down to different ways of estimating the utilization.

Hop Utilization: Practical Application

If your eyes glaze over looking at IBU equations – here's a practical guide. Hop utilization increases with boil time, so the longer you boil your hops the more bitterness and IBUs you will add. Late addition hops (boiled for 5-10 minutes) add very little bitterness, and are used primarily for aroma. Bittering hops are usually added for the full boil time (60-90 minutes).

Hop utilization also increases as you lower the gravity of your boil. If you are brewing a high gravity beer, or an extract brewer using a partial batch boil (small pot) you will get much lower utilization. This is why extract brewing requires more hops (in general) than all-grain brewing. Since different brewers use different equipment, it is important to take into account your own boil size and boil gravity when estimating the bitterness of your beer.

IBU Estimation

Three equations to estimate utilization (U%) and IBUs are most often used: Rager, Tinseth and Garetz. The equations differ in the way that they estimate the utilization percentage described earlier. Rager is most often associated with extract and partial mash brewers. The Rager equation takes original gravity of the boil into account, and tends to produce IBU estimates that are on the high side of the three equations.

Tinseth is often associated with all-grain brewers, or brewers that do full batch boils. It generally produces lower IBU estimates than Rager, but is considered very accurate. Many all grain brewers use Tinseth by default, though if using BeerSmith you can change this from the Options dialog. The Garetz equation is less popular than the other two methods, but generally provides estimates somewhere between Rager and Tinseth.

I won't go into the details of calculating each equation. A quick web search on any of these methods will yield a number of online calculators and spreadsheets. In addition, all major brewing software programs including my program BeerSmith offer the ability to estimate IBUs directly from the recipe. I recommend using a program or spreadsheet, as the complexity of multiple hop additions and late extract additions make it tedious to calculate by hand.

It's important to understand that the three estimation methods will provide widely varying results in some cases. Each provides only an estimate of bitterness, and none are perfect or all encompassing. I would not spend too much time worrying the differences. Choose a single estimation method and stick with it.

How Much Hops is Enough?

Now that we understand the basics of calculating IBUs, we come back to the original question of how much is enough? The answer varies by the style of beer we are targeting. The bitterness needed for an Imperial Stout is dramatically higher than a simple Pilsner. In general, beers with higher gravity need more bitterness to offset the maltiness of the beer. Similarly styles such as India Pale Ale where bitterness is a significant flavor component require more hops.

Fortunately, a number of beer style guides offer IBU ranges needed to achieve a particular beer style. The Beer Judge Certification Program (BJCP) maintains the most widely used US style guide. The 2008 BJCP Style Guide provides detailed

IBU ranges for dozens of popular beer styles from around the world. Other countries also have beer style guides that provide similar information. Programs like BeerSmith have the style guide built in for easy reference when designing a recipe.

Let's look at a BJCP example: From the standard, an American Amber Ale should have between 20 and 40 IBUs. If we target the middle of the range, 30 IBUs is about right. Using a spreadsheet or brewing software, it's easy to adjust your hops quantity and boil times to reach that target.

Balancing your Beer with the Bitterness Ratio

The balance between bitter hops and sweet malts has always been important in crafting world class beer. Here, we take a look at the bitterness ratio and how you can use it to improve the balance of homebrewed beer recipes.

The sweetness of malted barley and specialty grains must be offset by bitterness. Early beers used all kinds of herbs including ginger, caraway, cinnamon, citron, coriander, juniper, mint, myrtle, saffron, hysop, dill, thistles, and many others to counterbalance the sweetness of malt. Most modern beers use hops for bitterness, though some specialty beers like Belgian Wit still make use of other spices.

The Bitterness Ratio

The idea of trying to quantify the hop bitterness to sweet malt balance is also not new. English brewers regularly used "pounds of hops per quarter of malt" over the last several hundred years to characterize the hops-malt balance. Modern brewers started using the modern equivalent, called the bitterness ratio or BU:GU ratio many years ago. The measure, determined by simply dividing the number of IBUs in a beer by the number of gravity units, provides a rough estimate of the balance between hop bitterness and malt sweetness. It is featured in Ray Daniel's Designing Great Beers book where he lists the average bitterness ratio for many popular styles.

To calculate the bitterness ratio we start with the number of international bitterness units or IBUs. For example, let's say we start with a beer that has 30 IBUs and original gravity of 1.048. We take the fractional portion of the original gravity (0.048) and multiply by 1000 to get the number of gravity points. In this example 1.048 would simply be 48 points. Now we take 30 IBUs and divide by 48 points to get a bitterness ration of 0.63. If you are using BeerSmith, the estimated bitterness ratio (IBUs/OG points) is displayed just below the color on the recipe design page.

The Bitterness Ratio and Beer Styles

Obviously the bitterness ratio needed varies depending on the style of the beer. A hoppy India Pale Ale is going to have a much higher target bitterness ratio than a barely hopped Weizenbier. To determine the correct target bitterness ratio, one needs to know the average IBUs and starting gravity for different beer styles. Fortunately, the BJCP style guideline provides just such a resource. To calculate your target average style BU:GU ration, determine the average IBUs for the style guide and divide by the average OG points for the style. I've calculated the average bitterness ratio for a few popular styles here from the 2008 BJCP guidelines:

- American Amber: 0.619
- Bohemian Pilsner: 0.800
- Oktoberfest/Marzen: 0.449
- Traditional Bock: 0.346
- Blonde Ale: 0.467
- California Common: 0.735
- Ordinary Bitters: 0.833
- American Pale Ale: 0.714
- Brown Porter: 0.576
- Dry Irish Stout: 0.872
- English IPA: 0.800
- Weizen/Weissbier: 0.240

- Belgian Trippel: 0.375

The above is just a sampling, but gives us some idea of the range of average bitterness ratios for different styles. A higher bitterness ratio corresponds to more bitter beers overall. Not surprisingly many of the malty or high wheat German beers such as Weizen and Bock have low average bitterness ratios (0.240-0.345), while IPAs, Pale Ales, and those with high concentrations of dark malt such as stouts have much higher average ratios of 0.800 or higher. Other popular styles lie in the middle range of around 0.500, such as Oktoberfest, Porter, and Blonde Ale.

The bitterness ratio does not tell the whole story, as it does not take into account the individual grains making up the grain bill. For example Oktoberfest/Marzen has a malty flavor from its Munich malt grain bill base that is not reflected in its mid-range BU:GU ratio. Irish Stout, which requires a higher BU:GU ratio to balance its high concentration of black/stout roast malt has a relatively high 0.872 bitterness ratio, but the dry flavor of the roasted malt dominates the flavor profile over hops bitterness.

Calculating the bitterness ratio for a given beer and comparing it to the average for your target beer style can help to create a beer with an appropriate flavor balance, especially when traditional ingredients are used. I personally like to do a sanity check on my bitterness ratio against the style guide to make sure I'm in the ballpark when creating a new recipe.

Ten Reasons to Use Home Brewing Software

Many homebrewers are not aware of how brewing software can dramatically improve the quality and consistency of their home brew. Brewing without doing the math is kind of like shooting darts blindfolded, and software makes the math much easier. Here, we take a look at some of the ways brewing software like BeerSmith can make a difference in beer design and how it can improve your brewing day.

- **Design Great Beer in Minutes** – Building a recipe with beer software is as simple as picking the ingredients you want from a list. A typical package has several hundred varieties of hops, grains, yeasts and more that are pre-entered for your use. Picking from a list of ingredients is much easier than thumbing through a set of reference books and tables.
- **Brew Consistently Good Beer** – By tracking your ingredients, recipe used, original gravity and taste of your beer you can improve your brewing process and make more consistent, better tasting beer. You can keep track of old recipes, see how changes affect your color, gravity and bitterness, and design better beers.
- **Brew the Style you Want** – Brewing software lets you select a target beer style and match the color, bitterness and suggest ingredients as you build the recipe. As you add ingredients, the software estimates each of these and lets you compare the current values to the style you selected. This will help you come much closer to your target beer style the first time out.
- **Share Recipes** – Brewing software that supports open standards like BeerXML give you access to thousands of recipes online that you can download, import and customize to your taste. Many of the popular packages have dedicated recipe sites available. You can also email recipes to your friends, post them on a web site or share them in a variety of formats.
- **Get Step by Step Instructions** – Software like BeerSmith will generate step-by-step instructions customized for your recipe, equipment and methods. No fuss, no worries. After you enter your recipe you can get specific brewing instructions generated by the program with a single click.

- **Stay Organized** – Keep all of your brewing records in one place. Keep a brewing log of your past brewing sessions, schedule your next brew, record new ideas and manipulate recipes from the web. Refine your favorite recipes to perfect your brewing technique.

- **Match your Brewing Equipment** – The equipment you use to brew has a huge impact on the taste of your beer. With brewing software you can set up your equipment settings once and apply that to any recipe to get accurate calculations and estimates.

- **All Grain Made Easy** – Modern equipment and ingredients have made all grain brewing more accessible than ever. Infusion mashing for all-grain brewing involves a fairly complex set of calculations to determine the amount and temperature of water to be added at each step. In BeerSmith, you just pick the infusion profile you desire and the software provides detailed instructions that match your equipment and ingredients.

- **Manage Inventory, Track Prices and go Shopping** – The best brewing software includes tools to manage your inventory of ingredients, determine the cost of each brew and even generate shopping lists for a particular recipe for your next trip to the store. This makes it much easier to keep track of what you need and avoid those extra trips to the store.

- **Software Costs Less than a Batch of Beer** – Brewing software is cheap – typically from $20-30 for the top commercial packages. One bad tasting batch of beer costs more.

Converting All Grain Recipes to Extract

As an extract brewer and beer designer, you may quickly find that many of the beer recipes in books and on the web are designed by all grain brewers. Beginning brewers start with extract recipes but serious enthusiasts eventually make the switch to all-grain. Yet it is the expert brewers who write all of the brewing books and publish a large portion of recipes online. This can leave many extract brewers out in the cold.

Fortunately you can convert all grain recipes into extract recipes, often with very good results. The basic process for converting an all grain recipe to extract is as follows:

- Convert the base malt (usually pale malt grains) to an equivalent amount of extract
- Adjust the color of the beer down to match the original color
- Dial the hops up to match the IBUs of the original recipe

Converting a recipe is best done with the aid of brewing software or a good spreadsheet since you need to be able to adjust the original color, IBUs and original gravity estimates. At the end of the article, I will cover exactly how to do this using BeerSmith in a single step.

Converting Grains to Malt Extract

For the first step, convert your base malt to extract. The base malt is easy to identify, as it is the largest ingredient in the beer – typically 5-10 lbs (2.3-4.5 kg) of pale malt. For example, let's look at an all-grain ale with 8 lbs of pale malt and 1 lb of crystal malt. The simplest base malt conversion is to just multiply the number of pounds of pale maletby 0.75 to get the pounds of liquid extract. Therefore, 8 pounds (3.6 kg) of pale malt becomes 6 pounds (2.7 kg) of liquid extract.

An equivalent conversion for dry extract is 0.6, so 8 pounds (3.6 kg) of pale malt becomes 4.8 pounds (2.2 kg) of dry malt. A more accurate conversion would actually take the potential of the grain and extract into account when converting malt, but this level of precision is rarely needed.

To simplify things, we leave the specialty malts (1 lb of crystal) alone and switch to steeping them instead of mashing them. Some specialty malts (notably wheats, Munich malt, flaked and terrified grains) cannot be steeped and need to be replaced with a reasonable substitute. For example, those grains listed in our online grain listing as "must mash" should not be steeped. The same is true if you have a large proportion of specialty malt.

A good rule of thumb is you should steep no more than 3-5 lbs (1.3-2.3 kg) of specialty grains in the final extract recipe. Obviously you want to choose your malt extract to match the original color and style of the beer. If you are converting a wheat beer, choose a wheat extract. Beers with large amounts of Munich malt require a Munich extract. If you are making a light colored beer, pick the palest extract you can find. Pale extract is always a good starting point.

Matching Beer Color

Once you have your base malt converted, the next step is to match your color. Malt extracts are significantly darker than the equivalent pale malt due to darkening in extract production and storage, so you will need to reduce the color and quantity your specialty malts to match the same color as the original beer.

To manually calculate the color of both your original beer and the final beer you can refer to the section on beer color. However, I recommend using your favorite brewing software or a spreadsheet to simplify the process.

If you don't have home brewing software, the best way to match the color of the original is really by trial and error. You can swap the existing specialty grains with lighter color grains (try 40L Crystal as a substitute for 60L Crystal malt for example), or you can reduce the amount of your darker colored specialty grains until you match the color of the original recipe.

Some very light colored beer styles such as Koelsch may be impossible to precisely match using malt extract simply because commercial malt extracts are much darker than equivalent pale malt grains. In these cases, try to get as light as you can and consider using malts such as Carafoam (if appropriate) to replace crystal malts if appropriate to further reduce the color.

Adjusting Bitterness

The last step is to match the bitterness (IBUs) of the original beer. When going from all grain to extract this involves adding more hops because partial batch boils result in lower hop utilization than full batch boils used by all grain brewers. Some use a rule of thumb such as "add 20% more hops" but it is far more accurate to calculate and match the IBUs for both versions.

Again a spreadsheet or program is needed to calculate the International Bitterness Units (IBUs) of the original beer and final beer. Don't use HBU's (Home Bitterness Units) here since the boil sizes between all grain and extract brews are much different. Before starting, make sure you have the correct boil size both for the original beer and converted recipe set correctly when calculating IBUs. All grain brewers use full size boils of 6+ gallons (23 l) for a 5 gallon (19 l) brew, while extract brewers use much smaller boils of 2-3 gallons (7.6-11.3 l) for 5 gallons (19 l) of beer. This has a large effect on hop utilization in the IBU calculation.

Once you have both calculations set up, simply increase the hop additions incrementally until you reach your target bitterness. You now have an extract beer recipe that will closely match your all grain recipe.

You can use the above three step guide with any brewing software or well designed spreadsheet to manually perform the three steps (convert base malt, adjust color, adjust bitterness).

If you wish to convert back (extract to all grain), you can follow the same three steps, but this time divide by the conversion factor: 6 lbs (2.7 kg) of pale extract/0.75 = 8 lbs (3.6 kg) of pale malt.

BeerSmith has a nice conversion wizard built in to do all three steps in one shot. Open the recipe you want converted, click on the 'Convert Recipe' toolbar button. Select the type (All Grain, Extract, Partial Mash) of conversion you wish to perform. Pick the target equipment profile you wish to convert to (since your extract equipment likely has a much smaller boil pot) and press the OK button. The program will perform all three steps and give you the finished recipe. It is a very handy feature if you have recipes from a book or the web that you wish to convert quickly.

Chapter 4: Partial Mash and All Grain Brewing

*"Always do sober what you said you would
do drunk. That will teach you to keep your
mouth shut." – Ernest Hemingway*

After you have mastered the art of brewing with malt extracts, the next step is to move to partial mash or all grain brewing. Both of these brewing methods add a step called "mashing" which converts barley grain and other specialty grains directly into wort. In the partial mash method, a mix of mashed grains and malt extract is used, while with the all grain method, no malt extract is used and the beer is entirely made from malted grain.

One decision extract brewers face is whether to move to partial mash brewing, which requires less equipment, or jump straight to all grain brewing. While partial mash brewing offers most of the advantages of all grain, the process takes just as long and is moderately complex. All grain brewing requires a bit more equipment, but using modern techniques can actually be easier to do in the long run. In recent years, many brewers have decided to make the direct jump to all grain without even brewing a partial mash beer.

Mashing Demystified

Mashing can be a mystical process for first time all-grain or partial mash beer brewers. At its heart, the mashing process uses hot water and natural enzymes to convert complex sugars from malt into simpler sugars that can be readily fermented by yeast.

To mash malted barley, all you need to do is immerse the barley in hot water and raise its temperature to a narrow range between 148-158F (64-70C), and hold the hot grain mixture there for 30-60 minutes. Then slowly drain the hot liquid from the bottom of your mash tun while adding hot water to the top in a process known as sparging or lautering to collect the wort you will boil with hops to make beer.

Several enzymes that naturally occur in barley malt play key roles in breaking down these sugars. We'll cover all of the enzymes in a future section, but for the moment we're most concerned about two enzymes called alpha and beta amylase.

These two enzymes, which are active in the temperature range between approximately 148-158F (64-70 C) do the bulk of the heavy cutting when it comes to breaking long strings of sugars into smaller strings that yeast can digest.

Mashing can be divided into temperature steps. Most brewers perform a single step infusion mash, which means they heat the water to one temperature (a single step) and hold it there while the conversion takes place. Advanced brewers add additional mash steps depending on the style of beer and flavor profile they are targeting.

The "infusion mash" means that you infuse hot water at a pre-calculated temperature to achieve your target step temperature, which for a single step mash is always in the range between 148-158F (64-70 C).

So a single step infusion mash involves adding hot water to your malted grains to raise it to a predetermined temperature, which you then hold for 30-90 minutes for the conversion to take place. For both partial mash and all grain brewing, we're going to use this single step infusion mash to create the wort we'll boil and ferment to make beer.

Partial Mash Brewing

Partial mash beer brewing provides an intermediate step for those experienced with extract brewing, but not yet ready to make the investment to brew all grain beer. Here we take a look at how to do partial mash brewing using equipment already available in the average kitchen.

Extract brewers have access to a fairly broad set of ingredients, but there are a number of specialty grains that do require mashing for proper use. Examples include wheats, Munich malt, Vienna malt, flaked barley, and many high protein adjuncts. Brewing authentic wheat beers, German beers and specialty beers require mashing.

While many brewers make the direct leap to all grain brewing, partial mash brewing techniques provide a great intermediate step to achieve the benefits of all grain mashing without the investment in large amounts of new equipment. Here we're going to look at countertop partial mash techniques that minimize the need for extra equipment.

Partial Mash Equipment

Countertop partial mash brewing starts with the same equipment you used for extract brewing. In addition you need a grain bag is to contain the grains or a strainer to separate them. Partial mash brewers can also use a small, clean drink or picnic cooler to hold the temperature of the mash steady during the mash process.

The Partial Mash Method

In partial mashing, only a portion of the grains required for an all grain beer are mashed, while the bulk of the wort is made from malt extract. Typically only a few pounds of specialty grains plus a small amount of pale malt are actually mashed, and then the runnings of the mash are mixed with malt extract and boiled to produce the beer.

When formulating a partial mash recipe, you need to have a combination of the specialty malts needed for the beer plus a few pounds of pale malt. The pale malt is needed to provide the critical enzymes needed for mashing, as specialty grains do not normally contain these enzymes.

The mashing process converts long, complex sugar molecules into shorter ones that yeast can consume. For mashing, a combination of grains and water must be mixed together and held at a constant temperature range between 148-158F (64-70C) – ideally around 154 F (68C). The challenge is to maintain a constant temperature for the time it takes the mashing to complete – typically 30-60 minutes.

Two methods are typically used to maintain temperature. One is to heat the mash mixture over a stove and attempt to regulate the heat to hold a constant temperature. A second method, called infusion mashing, simply heats a pre-measured quantity of water and mixes it with the grains in an insulated container like a small cooler, relying on the insulation of the cooler to maintain a constant temperature.

I've tried both methods, and I strongly prefer using a cooler. Maintaining a constant temperature within just a few degrees over a typical stove is very difficult. Further if you overshoot your target temperature by a significant amount you can bring the mashing process to a halt resulting in an incomplete conversion of the sugars.

For infusion mashing, place your crushed grains in a grain bag and determine the correct amount and temperature of water to add. Typically 1.2-1.7 quarts of water are added per pound of grain (2.5-3.5 l/kg). Then the entire mixture is put in an insulated cooler. The temperature of water needed can be calculated using the BeerSmith infusion tool or an online infusion calculator. Preheat the water, add it to your cooler, and then add the grain bag and seal the top to maintain a constant temperature for 30-60 minutes.

The Iodine Test

You can confirm that the mash is complete with a small amount of iodine from the local drug store. Pull a small amount of liquid wort from the mash, and add a few drops of iodine. If the added iodine turns clear, then the mash is complete. If it is still dark blue, then the mash is not complete.

Once complete, simply slowly remove the grain bag from the mash. Add the resulting hot liquid to your boil pot, mix in your malt extract and top it off with water to proceed with the boil, cooling and fermentation just as you would with any normal extract beer.

All Grain Mashing

All grain beer brewing has become the most popular brewing style for intermediate to advanced home brewers. About 70% of regular home brewers now use all grain methods. In this section, we'll cover methods for all grain beer brewing using a single step infusion mash setup. Infusion mashing with a Gott type cooler, will unleash the full power of all grain brewing while keeping it simple.

Equipment Needed

To brew all grain beer, you need some new equipment. This includes a 7-9 gallon (27-34 l) brew pot and a 5 gallon (19 l) or 10 gallon (38 l) Gott type water cooler with a false bottom. I personally use a Phils false bottom (9" diameter) in my cooler and drain using a hose that runs through the removed tap for the cooler. A properly sized stopper can be inserted with a plastic tube where the tab was so you can drain liquid from the bottom of the cooler via the false bottom.

In addition to the cooler/mash tun, you will need a large pot suitable for boiling 6+ gallons (22 l) of water for a 5 gallon (19

l) batch. I personally recommend a 7-9 gallon (27-34 l) pot, as the beer will tend to foam and you need space above the actual wort to avoid boiling over. For your large pot, I also recommend purchasing an inexpensive propane burner as it is difficult to boil such a large pot over your stove. Most all grain brewers use large "turkey type" propane burners outside, as it will boil a large pot quickly.

Infusion Mashing

The infusion mash process is remarkably similar to the process we used for partial mash. Crush all of your grains in a grain mill first. The grain should be finely ground, but the husks of the grain should be relatively intact as the husks act as a filter in the grain bed. Next, heat a pre-measured amount of water, called an infusion, to a target temperature and mix it with the grains. This infusion step (mashing process) breaks down complex sugars in the crushed grain and converts it to simple sugars that can be fermented by yeast.

You can use one of many spreadsheets, online calculators or a brewing program such as BeerSmith to calculate the temperature and amount of infusion water needed for the mash. Make sure you use the correct equipment settings and total grain amount in the calculation. If using BeerSmith, make sure you have your equipment set up to include the water cooler as your mash tun and choose a "Single Infusion, Medium Body, No Mash Out" as your mash profile. Use a target step temperature of 154F (68 C), which is an excellent mid-range temperature for your first infusion mash.

Heat the recommended amount of infusion water to the temperature provided by your calculator or brewsheet. Slowly alternate adding water and grain to your mash tun until you have all of the water and grains mixed together. Insert a thermometer so you can track the temperature against your target step temperature. Close the top and let your mash temperature settle for 5-10 minutes.

Slowly mix your mash every 10-15 minutes to keep the temperature even and avoid hotspots. The mash mixture should reach a steady temperature close to 154F (68 C). If it is off by a significant amount, you can add a small amount of boiling or cold water to achieve the target temperature. Leave your mash mixture in the cooler for at least 45 minutes to assure that the sugar conversion is complete.

Sparging and Lautering

In the sparging (also called lautering) step, you run hot water slowly through the grain bed in your mash tun and extract the wort from the bottom of the bed, where it then runs down into your boiler.

After 45 minutes of mashing, sparge the mash with hot water to extract the sweet wort that will be your beer. Sparging is nothing more than rinsing the grains with hot water to extract the sugars and create wort.

Heat several gallons of water to 170F (77 C) and slowly add it to the top of your mash tun while drawing wort from the bottom of the grain tun using your false bottom and collect it in your boiler. The wort coming from the mash tun will start out cloudy with bits of grain and husks, but will soon run clear. Take the first few quarts of wort drained from the tun (the first runnings) and add them back to the top of your mash tun to reduce the cloudy grain bits.

As you continue to sparge, it is important to keep the flow rate slow to maximize the sugars extracted. Lautering a 5 gallon (19 l) mash tun should take at least 30-40 minutes to collect 6 gallons (23 l) of wort. From this point forward, the process used to brew your beer is the same as it was with extract brewing. Add hops, boil the wort for 60-90 minutes, cool it quickly to room temperature and add your yeast to ferment your beer.

Switching to single infusion all grain brewing is a great way to gain more control over your beer, and requires only a little bit of additional and time. The single infusion mash provides a good starting point for those transitioning to all grain. Take the leap, and enjoy brewing your first all grain today!

Understanding Brewhouse Efficiency

Brewhouse efficiency is a term that causes some confusion for first time all grain brewers. When you start designing partial mash or all grain beers, you will need to understand brewhouse efficiency and how it to calculate it to get the right amount of grains into your recipe.

Brewhouse efficiency is defined as the percent of potential grain sugars that are converted into sugar in the wort. Typically this includes losses for a given brewing setup, and these losses are taken in aggregate rather than accumulated individually. It is therefore a measure of the overall efficiency of your brewing system.

Brewhouse efficiency is a key input when designing all grain recipes, as it determines your estimated original gravity. If you don't have an accurate brewhouse efficiency number for your particular equipment setup, your original gravity estimates will be way off and you will miss your target gravity.

Brewhouse Efficiencies for Grains

Every grain in an all grain recipe has a potential yield, listed as the dry grain fine yield on the malt sheet. The dry grain yield is determined in laboratory conditions, by powdering the grain and then extracting maximum potential from the sample. Yields vary from 50%-87% depending on the type of grain used. You can also express yield as a potential such as 1.038.

The actual brewhouse efficiency is measured for an entire system. Unlike the dry grain yield or potential measured in a lab, real brewers achieve only a percentage of the ideal number due to real considerations such as efficiency of the mashing process, and losses due to boiling, deadspace or trub. This percentage of the potential, as measured across the whole system into the fermenter, is the brewhouse efficiency.

A related term is mash efficiency. Unlike brewhouse efficiency, mash efficiency measures only the efficiency of the mash and sparging steps. Mash efficiency can be through of as the percent of potential fermentables extracted during the mashing process that actually make it into the boiler.

Calculating Efficiencies

Programs such as BeerSmith will calculate the brewhouse efficiency from a given recipe, volume and original gravity, but it is useful to understand the underlying equations. Let's look first at how to calculate the total potential of the grain for a batch of beer:

(potential_pts) = (grain_pts) * (weight lbs) / volume_gals

Each grain has a dry grain potential, which you can find from our grain listing or from the malter's web site. The grain_pts is calculated from the grain potential by subtracting 1.000 and multiplying by 1000. For example, a grain with a potential of 1.035 becomes simply 35 points. 5 pounds (2.3 kg) of this grain in a 5 gallon (19 l) batch would add 35*5/5 = 35 potential points to the beer.

If we sum all of the potential points from the various grain additions we can get the overall potential. If we had no losses in the system, the 35 points above would give an ideal starting gravity for our beer of 1.035.

I mentioned that the potential points represent the gravity under ideal laboratory conditions. In practice one gets much less than this, usually around 70-80% for brewhouse efficiency overall. Therefore the potential points times the gravity determine the actual original gravity:

(batch_pts) = (potential_pts) * (brewhouse efficiency)

So if we consider a recipe with 40 potential points, and a 75% brewhouse efficiency we get 30 batch points or an original gravity of 1.030. This is how original gravity is estimated.

Reversing the calculation we can calculate the efficiency from an ideal recipe potential estimate (potential_pts) and actual measurement (measured_pts).

(efficiency) = (measured_pts) / (potential_pts)

So for example if we had a recipe with potential_pts of 80 and measured the wort into the fermenter 1.050 we get an efficiency of 50/80 = 62.5%. Note that this assumes we hit our target volume. If we don't, we need to consider the target and actual volume as follows:

(efficiency) = (measured_pts * target_vol) / (potential_pts * actual_vol)

The formulas above give us the overall brewhouse efficiency, but can also be used to calculate the mash efficiency into the boiler. For efficiency into the boiler we simply use the boiler volume and measured boil specific gravity into the boiler as opposed to the fermenter. In BeerSmith you can click on the "brewhouse efficiency" button in any open recipe to perform more detailed mash or overall efficiency calculations including those shown above.

Now you know how to calculate the two key all grain efficiencies: brewhouse and mash efficiency. In the next section, we'll talk about how to improve your efficiency.

Improving your Brewhouse Efficiency

All grain brewers can be obsessive about the efficiency of their brewing system. Now that we've defined brewhouse efficiency, we will look at 5 methods you can use to improve your overall brewhouse efficiency.

Achieving higher efficiency on a consistent basis lets you use fewer grains to achieve a target original gravity. All grain brewers, particularly those who are inexperienced, often have low efficiency numbers. Let's look at five ways to increase your efficiency number:

1. Improve the Milling of your Grains

The crush of your grains makes a significant difference in the efficiency of your mash and sparge. Grains should be finely crushed, but the milling should leave the hulls largely intact to act as a filter bed. A dual roller mill such as the Barley Crusher is ideal for achieving this. Note that if you crush your grains too finely you will plug up your filter bed resulting in a "stuck mash". In a "stuck mash", the filter bed will clog up and the wort will stop flowing.

2. Mash Out or Sparge with Hot Water

Hot water during the mash out and sparge helps the sticky wort flow more freely. Ideally you would like to raise the mash temperature to about 168F (77 C) and then use 168F (77 C) water to sparge. A mash out infusion addition can be used to help raise the temperature of your mash as you sparge. However you should avoid raising your mash temperature above 175F as it could result in excess tannin extraction.

3. Sparge Slowly

Most beginners attempt to sparge their mash much too fast. Sparging too quickly leaves insufficient time for the hot water to extract the sugars in the grain bed. Limit the flow out of your mash tun to just above a trickle. It should take 30-50 minutes to fully sparge a 5 gallon (19 l) all grain batch (about 6 gallons of wort).

4. Minimize Losses in your System

Losses anywhere in your brewing system, including deadspace in the mash tun, transfer lines, pumps, and trub at the end of the mash result in lost wort. The lost wort takes sugars with it, reducing your overall brewhouse efficiency. Use a properly sized mash tun, and work to eliminate deadspace in the system.

5. Pick a Properly Designed Mash Tun

The design of your mash tun and false bottom or screen can have a huge effect on the efficiency of the mash process. A round, cylindrical mash tun is generally considered best, as it leaves the depth of the grain bed about equal to its width. This is one reason cylindrical water coolers are popular.

The false bottom ideally will cover the entire bottom of the mash tun but have minimal deadspace underneath it. This will provide an even flow across the entire grain bed giving better efficiency.

Chapter 5: Hops and Hop Techniques

God made yeast as well as dough, and loves
fermentation just as dearly as he loves
vegetation" – Ralph Waldo Emerson

In earlier chapters we covered yeast and the importance of a yeast starter as well as how to use various types of malted grain in your extract or all grain beer. Now we turn to the very important topic of hops. Hops provide bitterness in beer to offset the sweet flavor of the malt. Hops can be used in a variety of ways, so we're going to devote this entire chapter to hop techniques.

Hop Aging and Hop Storage

With hop prices running high, caring for your precious hops supply is more important than ever. Here we're going to look at the best way to store and preserve your hops and also some of the effects of hop aging.

Hop Aging and the Enemies of Hops

All hops will age over time. Precious hop oils including both aromatic and bittering oils tend to break down over time, and old hops will lose aroma, flavor and bitterness as they age. Stale hops will take on a cheesy or skunky flavor that can ruin your beer. Hops have three main enemies: heat, light and oxygen.

Heat accelerates the chemical breakdown of hops including both aromatic oils and the alpha acids that provide most of the bitterness in beer. The relationship between temperature and hop bitterness is exponential – hop aging is cut in half for every 15 degrees C (27 F) of lowered temperature. Hops stored at 75F (24 C) will degrade almost 4 times as fast as hops stored in a freezer. To slow the aging of your hops, always store them in the freezer at a temperature between 30F and -5F (-1 to -21 degrees C).

Light is also a natural enemy of hops. Hop cones are susceptible to breakdown from sunlight from the first minute they are picked, so hop growers go to great lengths to make sure that hops are not exposed to sunlight after picking. When possible, store your hops in a dark place and avoid exposure to sunlight.

Oxygen is also an enemy of hops because hop oils and alpha acids will oxidize. Oxidized alpha acids lose their bitterness, and old hops will take on a "cheesy" aroma. A plastic/poly bag is the worst storage vessel for your hops because plastic bags are still permeable to air. You can smell the hops right through a typical plastic bag, which is an indicator that it is not much of an oxygen barrier.

An oxygen barrier bag or an airtight jar makes a much better container, though these still typically contain some air. The best container is a vacuum sealed oxygen barrier such as a vacuum packed foil pouch, typically made from a layer of food grade plastic and layer of mylar.

Note that whole hops degrade faster because of the larger surface area exposed to air. Most hop processors will at some point pelletize their aging hops because the highly compressed pellets age more slowly than whole hops. Pellets also take less space and are easier to vacuum pack, which is why they are often used in homebrewing and microbrewing.

Hop Storage Index: How Long Can I Store My Hops?

The speed of aging varies by hop variety. The aging rate for a particular variety is measures using the Hop Storage Index (HSI), which is the amount of hops alpha acid potential lost in 6 months when the hops are stored at a constant temperature of

68 F (20 C). Hops will last over three times as long as their HSI would indicate if frozen and stored properly.

For example a hops with a starting alpha of 10% and HSI of 25% stored for 6 months would lose 25% of its alpha potential, resulting in a new alpha rating of 7.5% if stored at 68F (20 C). The same hops stored for 6 months at 28F (-2C) would only lose 10% of its alpha acids leaving it at 9% alpha content. To see sample HSI ratings for various hop varieties, visit our hops listing on my web site and click on the hop variety of interest. The HSI is on the detailed page for each hops near the bottom. (see the support page on **BeerSmith.com** for a link to our hop listing).

The HSI does not tell the whole story however. Hops will age at a much slower rate if stored in cold temperature and in a proper container. BeerSmith has a Hop Aging tool (Tools menu) you can use to calculate a particular variation of hop packaging, temperature and age, and also has the HSI in its hops database so you can just pick a hop variety, set your storage conditions and calculate the resulting alpha.

Which brings us to the final question – how long can you store your hops without ill flavor effects? It turns out the lower alpha aromatic hop oils are the most susceptible to aging, so if you are looking for a burst of aromatics with hops added at the end of the boil or for dry hopping, choose fresh hops.

You can use the HSI or detailed hop aging tool as a guide as follows: Hops are considered "bad" by commercial growers when they drop below 50% of their original alpha acid content. At this point, the hops typically take on a "cheesy" aroma, and should be discarded. I will note that even "poor" HSI hops with 50% HSI will last the better part of a year if stored properly in a freezer and oxygen barrier bag.

An Overview of Hop Techniques

A good understanding of various hop techniques is critical for successful brewing. Yet the wide array of hopping techniques with terms such as mash hopping, first wort hops, dry hops, boil hops, and late hop additions can be confusing to first time and experienced brewers alike.

Beginners and intermediate brewers alike often apply the wrong technique to a given beer style. Knowing which technique to use for a particular style or desired flavor profile is part art form, but it all starts with a firm understanding of the techniques themselves.

I'll present the most common hop methods in something of a chronological order, starting with the mash and ending with finished beer:

Mash Hopping

Mash hopping is the addition of hops directly to the mash tun itself. The hops are often placed on top of the grain bed and left to sit as the mash is sparged. Mash hopping is reported to provide a better overall balance and character to the beer, though it adds almost no bitterness.

Mash hopping is seldom used today because it requires a fairly large amount of hops and adds very little in direct flavor. Since the hops are never boiled, no bitterness is released and most of the flavorful oils from the hop flower are lost in the boil that follows.

Brewers today theorize that most of the reported benefits from mash hopping are a byproduct of lower pH from mash hopping and not the hops itself. Given that many cheaper methods exist for controlling the pH of your wort, I'm not sure why a homebrewer would choose to mash hop.

First Wort Hops

First wort hops are hops added to the boil pot at the very start of the lautering process. Unlike mash hops, first wort hops remain in the boiler during the boil and therefore do contribute bitterness to the wort.

First wort hopping is an old German method that has enjoyed a home brewing resurgence. In blind taste tests, beers brewed with this method are perceived as smoother, better blended and have less of a bitter edge and aftertaste. I have personally used this method with great success on a variety of beers where a smooth well balanced bitterness is desirable. I've even used it on lightly hopped styles as it helps to reduce the perceived bitterness without upsetting the malt-bitterness balance of the beer.

Bittering Hops

Bittering hops or boiling hops are just that – hops added for the bulk of the boil to add bitterness to the beer. Boiling hops releases the alpha acids that provide bitterness in your beer. The longer you boil your hops, the more bitterness you will add.

We discussed in an earlier chapter how to estimate the bitterness (IBUs) for boiled hops. In general, your bittering additions should be boiled for full length of your boil (typically 60-90 minutes) to extract as much bitterness per ounce of hops as possible. I will usually add my bittering hop addition at the beginning of the boil.

Late Hop Additions

Hops added in the last 5-15 minutes of the boil are called late hop additions. These hops are usually not added for bittering, though they do contribute a small amount of bitterness to the beer. The main purpose for late hop additions is to add aroma and aromatic hop oils to your beer.

In addition to bittering compounds, hop cones from "aromatic" hop varieties contain volatile hop oils that provide the strong flowery aromatic flavor and scent desirable in many hoppy beer styles. Unfortunately most of these compounds boil off within 10-20 minutes of adding the hops.

The Hop Back

A hop back is a device containing hops used inline between the boiler and chiller to infuse fragile hop oils and aroma directly into the hot wort before it is cooled and transferred to the fermenter. While a hop back does not add any significant bitterness to the beer, it can add great aroma to your finished beer. For more information see our section on the hop back.

Dry Hopping

Dry hopping is the addition of hops after the beer has fermented. Hops are typically added in the secondary fermenter or keg and left for a period of several days to several weeks. Dry hopping is used to add a hoppy aroma to the beer, as no bitterness is added with this method. Dry hopping is also used in many commercial beers.

Combining Hop Methods

Advanced brewers use a combination of hop additions to achieve a burst of hop aroma and flavor, particularly for hoppy styles like India Pale Ale. In fact, many true hopheads will add substantial first wort and boil hops, followed by multiple late hop additions and a final dose of dry hops.

Personally, I try to keep things simple, so I will typically add a single boil or first wort addition for bitterness, followed by a single late hop addition in the last 5-10 minutes of the boil to preserve aromatics and dry hopping if appropriate. If I'm looking to save on hops, I'll also try to use higher alpha bittering hops for the main boil hops and save my precious aromatics for the late addition and for dry hopping.

On non-hoppy styles, I'll choose to add a single bittering addition as first wort hops since I like the smooth blending perception this method produces.

First Wort Hopping

Brewing beer with First Wort Hops (FWH) is a method I have used extensively for beer brewing over the last few years to improve the character of many recipes. First wort hopping produces complex bitterness and aroma that is both smooth and pleasing to the pallet. The method has become quite popular with homebrewers and microbreweries over the last 10 years due to the pleasant and complex flavor produced.

The First Wort Hop Method

FWH involves adding a portion of the hops to the boiler at the very beginning of the sparging process, allowing these hops to steep as the sparging completes and remaining in the kettle throughout the boil. Add the hops to the boiler as soon as you have finished recirculating the first runnings.

First Wort Hopping is not a new method, but is in fact an old one from Germany that was largely forgotten until Priess, Neuremburg and Mitter published an article on it in 1995 (Brauwelt International, Vol IV, p 308). Brewers originally used the method at the beginning of the century to enhance bitterness rather than overall flavor. Adding hops to the wort early in the sparging process reduced the pH of the mash, which enhanced isomerization of later hop additions, increasing overall hop utilization during the boil.

Sources vary, but most testing indicates that first wort hopping will increase the number of International Bitterness Units (IBUs) by as much as 10%. However, taste perception is different. In blind taste testing across a number of articles, the overall flavor of first wort hops is perceived as smoother, less sharp, and had a more pleasing aroma. Hop bitterness was perceived as harmonic and uniformly bitter. In blind taste tests, the FWH were preferred by 11 of 12 test subjects.

First wort hopping can be used both by all grain and partial mash brewers. As the FWH method originated in Germany, it has most often been associated with Pilsner beers, but other beer styles with complex hop flavor could benefit. Aromatic, noble and other low alpha hops are recommended, as high alpha hops may provide too sharp of an increase in bitterness.

The amount to hops to use varies. Most sources recommend using 30% of the overall hop schedule and moving it to FWH. Other sources recommend taking aromatic hops from the end of the boil and moving it forward to use as FWH. I have even experimented on my Wit beer with using FWH exclusively and had good results. My experience indicates that if you are looking for a smooth pilsner style hoppiness, moving some or all of your boil hops forward is appropriate. FWH in general will produce a more complex, blended hop flavor.

Calculating the FWH numerically is quite simple. In most cases an adjustment (10%) is added to the calculated bitterness in IBUs to account for the higher utilization of FWH methods. For BeerSmith users, there is a checkbox for first wort hops available as you add each hop addition, and BeerSmith will adjust the IBU calculation to account for the higher utilization. Despite the slightly higher IBUs of FWH, most authors do not recommend reducing the overall hop rate to compensate.

Overall, I have been very pleased with the effect first wort hopping has had on my beers. I have taken to using it on a larger variety of beer styles recently with good results. FWH seems to produce a more complex and harmonic hop flavor and aroma that beer drinkers find pleasing.

Brewing with a Hop Back

Many micro and commercial brewers to add hoppy flavor and aroma to any beer use the "hop back". Homebrewers can also take advantage of this technique with simple equipment to add additional aroma to home brewed beer.

Using a Hop Back

A hop back is a device that is inserted in line as the beer is transferred and cooled from the hot boiler into the fermenter. The main purpose of a hop back is to transfer delicate hop oils and aromas that would otherwise be boiled off in the boiler. The technique is used for many ales and related styles where a hoppy aroma is desirable.

Whole or plug hops are used in a hop back, as the goal of the device is to maximize surface contact between the hot wort and the hops. Typically 1-2 oz (28-56 g) of hops are used for a 5 gallon (19 l) batch. The hop back is inserted at the hot end, closest to the boiler to maximize the transfer of hop oils. Little actual alpha bitterness is added by a hop back, as the wort is not boiling, but a lot of fragile hop oils and aromas can be added. Since aroma, and not bitterness, are the goal it is best to use low alpha aroma hop varieties such as noble hops in your hop back.

Commercial brewers often make dual use of the hops from their hop back. After the hops have been used in a hop-back, many of the fragile aromatic oils have been taken out but the high alpha bittering hop oils remain. Therefore brewers take the hops used in the hop back and boil them to extract bitterness in a subsequent batch. While this is difficult for homebrewers to do unless they brew multiple batches in a day, some homebrewers have been able to reuse hops in this way when creating parti-gyle brews (more than one batch of beer from a single mash).

You can purchase a small hopback device from many home brewing supply stores. These typically consist of a small watertight container that can be easily opened and sanitized before use. Hops are added to the container and it is sealed for use. An inlet tube and outlet tube flow the hot wort through the hop back, and then into either a counterflow chiller or other cooling device before the wort is transported to the fermenter.

Making your own Hop Back

You can also build a hop-back at home from most any watertight heat resistant container. One of the more innovative home designs I've seen consists of nothing more than a Ball canning jar with holes drilled into the top where tubes and fittings have been added to produce a watertight seal for an inlet and outlet tube. If you create such a device it is important to use lead-free solder when soldering the pieces together, and check the system to make sure it is watertight before use.

Using a hop back is a great way to add an extra burst of hop flavor and aroma to your favorite ale. It imparts many desirable aromatic oils, much like the dry hopping method we will cover next.

Dry Hopping: Enhance your Hop Aroma

Dry hopping is a great way to enhance the hoppy aroma of your home brewed beer. Real hopheads will tell you that in addition to boil and late hop additions, adding dry hops is a preferred technique for preserving a burst of delicate hop aroma for IPAs and other hoppy beers.

Dry Hopping

Dry hopping involves adding hops to the fermenter or keg after fermentation. Dry hops are allowed to soak in the finished beer for anywhere from several days to several weeks.

Commercial craft brewers use dry hopping to enhance their beer including Anchor Liberty, Samuel Adams Pale Ale and

Sierra Nevada celebration. Many drinkers prefer the distinctly floral hop aroma that dry hopping adds. On the con side, some drinkers perceive a "grassy" or "oily" flavor from dry hopping. The technique is appropriate for brewing beer styles with high hop rates such as IPAs, Pale Ales, some Stouts and California Common (Steam) beer.

Dry Hop Selection
The first question that arises when dry hopping is which hops to use? Aromatic hops with low alpha rates (6% or less) are considered preferable because these hops have a higher percentage of fragile aromatic hop oils needed for dry hopping. All of the noble hops as well as most of the low alpha aromatic varieties are appropriate.

Examples include: Saaz, Tettnanger, Hallertauer, Goldings, Fuggles, Cascade and Williamette. You should select hops that matches the origin and beer style – an English Goldings hops might be appropriate for an English Ale or India Pale Ale for instance.

The next question is what form of hops to use: pellets, plugs or whole hops? Plug or pellet hops are generally preferred, especially for those using a carboy with a narrow neck. Getting whole hops in and out of the fermenter can be difficult. Pellet hops can cause some foaming when added because, much like diet coke and mentos, the pellets have a large surface area that promotes nucleation of the CO_2 left from fermentation.

Some purists prefer plug hops as they fear that the extra processing and compression of pellet hops may have an effect on the delicate hop oils and aroma. Personally, I have noticed no significant difference between plug and pellet hops when dry hopping.

The amount of hops to use is largely a matter of preference. Between 1 and 2 oz (28-55g) per 5 gallons (19 L) is considered a moderate amount. Less can certainly be used if you are shooting for a mild floral aromatic, and true hopheads use as much as 4 oz (113 g) of hops for 5 gallons (19 l) for a burst of aroma.

Dry Hopping Methods

When should one add hops to the beer, and for how long? Some brewers add dry hops during primary fermentation, but most agree this can result in loss of precious hop aromas due to the steady stream of CO_2 bubbling out of the fermenter.

The appropriate time to add dry hops is after primary fermentation has completed. Adding dry hops to the secondary maximizes the exposure without risking volatile aromas. A third option is to add dry hops directly to the keg, but this can result in some "grassy" flavors from overexposure as the hops may remain in the keg for months.

Some brewers use a mesh bag to make it easier to contain the hops and make them easier to separate from the beer later. Others merely separate the beer from hops carefully when siphoning later. Pellets tend to sink after a while, while whole hops and plugs tend to float. Obviously a bag is required for kegging your hops to keep the hops from plugging the keg's outlet tube.

The duration of dry hopping also varies widely. An exposure of several days is the minimum needed to extract aromatic oils. Most brewers dry hop for between 5 and 14 days. Those that add hops to a keg may leave the hops in contact with the beer for months. Some fear overexposure will add a "grassy" flavor, but I've never had a significant problem with this. I personally recommend one week in the secondary.

Dry hopping is an important method for your homebrewing arsenal. Many of the hoppiest styles require dry hopping to achieve an appropriate balance and aroma for the finished beer.

Growing Hops at Home

No chapter on hops or hop techniques would be complete without a discussion of growing your own hops. Home brewers are turning in record numbers to growing hops for beer at home. Growing hops is a fun way to expand your personal hop supply. There is great pride of enjoying a beer brewed with home-grown hops.

Whether you live in the Northwest, Northeast, Midwest, South or California does not matter – hops can be grown in any moderate climate with proper care. Hops grow from small root-like cuttings about a foot long called rhizomes. It takes about two years to develop a mature hop bine from a rhizome, but you will get some hop cones the first season.

Rhizomes can be purchased from a variety of brewing suppliers online and mailed to your home – just do a quick search for "hop rhizomes" on the web.

Location for Growing Hops

Select an area with plenty of sun. Hops need at least 6-8 hours of sun a day, so the South facing side of your home or an exposed site is a good location. Hop vines (called bines) can grow to over 25 feet (7.62 m), so vertical space for a support trellis for the hop bines to climb is important.

Hops prefer well-aerated soil that is rich in nutrients and has good drainage. If you are going to plant several varieties, keep them well separated in your garden. Hop roots will spread quickly and take over the garden unless you separate them and trim the roots each season. Some brewers grow their hops in large pots or plastic containers to keep them from spreading.

Hop Planting and Care

Hops should be planted in the Spring, late enough to avoid a frost. Fertilize liberally before planting. Plant your hops in a mound and aerate the ground by turning it over several times to aid drainage, enhance growth and prevent disease. Place the rhizomes about 4 inches (10 cm) deep, and make your mound of soil about a foot high to aid drainage. Place the root side of the rhizome down. Cover the mound with some straw or light mulch to inhibit weeds.

The hop bines grow vertically and require some kind of trellis. Your trellis could consist of some heavy rope or twine going from ground level to your roof, or a few poles securely mounted in the ground. If using rope, select rough twine-like rope so the bines can grab onto it. Keep in mind that the hop bines can be 25+ feet (7.62 m) long and weigh 20+ pounds (9 kg). The trellis should be strong and secure.

Hops also enjoy lots of water and sunlight. In the dry climates or the heat of summer, they may need to be watered daily. Once the hop begins to grow, select the best bines and wrap them around your trellis to train them. You will need to train the hops for a few days, but eventually they will begin growing in a clockwise direction from east to west around your trellis. Train the best shoots and trim the rest off.

Harvesting and Drying your Hops
Your hops will continue to grow throughout the summer, and will be ready to harvest by late summer. The harvest in the first year may not be huge, and in fact it could be very small – hops don't reach peak yield until the second season of growth.

To determine when to harvest, you need to examine the cones. Mature hop cones will be dry to the touch, springy, have a very strong aromatic hop odor, and leave yellow lupulin powder on your fingers. Check the cones every day or two, and when you think they are ripe, pick one and open it. It should be filled with thick yellow-gold lupulin powder if it is fully ripened.

The hops may not all ripen at once, but you need to harvest each as it ripens. Dry the hops out in a warm dry spot in your house, and keep them away from sunlight. Sunlight can seriously damage picked hops. A paper bag is a good place to store them while drying. The hops should dry out in a week or two. After that, place them in a sealed bag and store the hop cones in your freezer. Remove as much oxygen as possible from the bag and ideally use some kind of oxygen barrier container to avoid oxidization.

Maintenance of Your Hops

Cut the bines back to 3 feet or so after harvesting. The winter frost will kill off the bines, after which you can cut them back further and cover the rhyzomes until Spring. The rhyzomes will go dormant for the winter. When Spring comes, take a spade and cut around the rhizome to trim the roots back to about a foot. Trimming the roots will prevent the hops from consuming your entire garden, as they tend to spread rapidly. Add some fertilizer, fresh mulch and a new trellis and you will be ready to grow hops for the new season.

Hop production typically reaches its peak after the second season; so don't be disappointed if your first year's yield is small. A properly cared-for hops garden will keep you in fresh hops for many years to come.

Chapter 6: All Grain Brewing

"I am a firm believer in the people. If given the truth, they can be depended upon to meet any national crisis. The great point is to bring them the real facts, and beer." –
Abraham Lincoln

We introduced the basics of all grain brewing using an infusion mash system in Chapter 4. In this chapter we will introduce more advanced techniques including the popular batch sparge method, recent "brew in a bag" method and advanced decoction mashing.

Fly Sparging vs. Batch Sparging

In this section, we'll look at traditional fly sparging, batch sparging and no-sparge brewing techniques. Batch sparge techniques have become very popular with homebrewers recently, primarily because batch sparging requires less time and less equipment than traditional techniques at minimal added cost.

Sparging Techniques

Recall that sparging (or lautering) is done at the end of the mash process, before the boil. The purpose is to extract the sugars created by the mashing process and dissolve them into hot water to form wort. We will then take the sugary wort, add some hops, boil it and ferment it to make our favorite beverage: Beer.

There are three techniques for sparging: the fly sparge, no sparge, and batch sparge. Traditionally, brewers use a fly sparge where hot sparge water is continuously sprayed over the top of the grain bed to replace the hot wort as it is drained from the bottom of the mash tun. This gives a continuous flow, ideally with the flow in matching the flow out. Commercial brewers will monitor the specific gravity of the hot wort coming out of the mash tun and stop when it reaches approximately 1.010 to avoid off flavors and tannins associated with low wort concentration.

Duplicating a traditional fly sparge at home does create some challenges for the homebrewer. One must have not only a method for spreading water continuously over the grain bed, but also constantly monitor the flow of the water into the mash tun to make sure the grain bed does not run dry or overflow. Also fly sparging is a slow process – requiring as much as 30-60 minutes in some cases.

Batch Sparge and No Sparge

Two alternatives to fly sparging are the "no sparge" and "batch sparge" techniques. For these techniques a fixed amount of hot sparge water is added to the mash tun, the tun is gently stirred to assure even extraction for the batch, and then the entire mash tun is drained into the boiler, often at a fast rate (i.e. just open the spigot). The "no sparge" option uses a higher water to grain ratio when mashing and drains it all out in a single operation, while batch spargers use two or more sparge water additions, draining the mash tun empty each time.

The downside of batch sparging is reduced brewhouse efficiency – since a significant amount of sugar will be left undissolved and be discarded with the grains rather than make its way into the wort. For example, a homebrewer fly sparging might achieve 73% brewhouse efficiency while a batch sparger might only get 66% brewhouse efficiency. Homebrewers compensate by adding more grain and just take the hit on efficiency.

For a commercial brewer the extra loss would be costly, but for the homebrewer making a 5 gallon (19 l) batch of beer adding

1-2 pounds (0.4-1 kg) of extra grain (perhaps $1-4 in cost) is not significant. For most homebrewers, the extra few dollars of grain is a good trade off when compared to the extra time and equipment needed to do a proper fly sparge. Batch sparging also has the advantage of higher gravity for the runnings, which will rarely come even remotely close to the 1.010 lower sparging limit mentioned earlier.

An additional concern with batch sparging is that stirring the mash upsets the grain bed, allowing more tannins and grain bits to make it into the wort. To reduce this risk, some brewers use a hybrid batch sparge method where they add sparge water slowly to the top and avoid stirring or completely draining the mash tun. This hybrid method does require additional time for the water to flow through the grain bed – much like a traditional fly sparge.

Batch sparging is more popular than no-sparge because it lets you use a traditional water to grain ratio when mashing, a smaller mash tun (typically a 5 gallon (19 l) mash tun for a 5 gallon batch), and achieves much higher efficiency than no sparge options.

Batch Sparge Calculations
The most popular is a two stage batch sparge with equal size batches (equal amount of wort drawn off, not equal amount of sparge water added). Two equal size runnings of wort (equal batches) also maximize the extraction efficiency. Calculating the amount of water to add for each sparge is straightforward where boil_size_l is your target boil size in liters, mash_water_l is the number of liters of mash water added and grain_wt_kg is the grain weight:

Two stage batch sparge additions:

batch_1_sparge_liters = (boil_size_l/2 – mash_water_l + grain_wt_kg * 0.625) batch_2_sparge_liters = boil_size_1 / 2

If you have deadspace under the mash tun, you must also add that amount of extra water to the first batch. If you have BeerSmith you can get an optimal "equal runnings" batch sparge that duplicates the sparge water calculations described above by selecting any of the default batch sparge mash profiles. The batch sparge amounts needed are displayed using the brewsheet (Preview Brewsheet) for your recipe.

The next item to consider is how much extra grain is required to use your batch sparge method. Unfortunately, it is difficult to know this in advance, since your mash efficiency will depend on the milling of your grain, efficiency of your lautering system and other factors. A good rule of thumb is to add about 10% to your grain bill (or alternately take about 7% off your starting overall brewhouse efficiency of the recipe) for the first try. Some people use this "rule of thumb" method to size their batch sparge grain bill.

If you use brewing software or a spreadsheet, you can calculate your overall brewhouse efficiency and use that number to properly size future batches. In BeerSmith, these calculations can be accessed from the "Brewhouse efficiency" button in the top section of any open recipe. This displays your estimated overall efficiency and OG in the "Brewhouse Efficiency based on Target Volume" section. Enter your actual volume into the fermenter and measured OG into the dialog and the program will calculate your actual overall brewhouse efficiency, which you can use for your next batch. After a few batch sparge trials you should have a good handle on what your brewhouse efficiency is, and you can then use the "scale recipe" command to adjust web recipes to your personal brewhouse efficiency.

Batch sparging is a great time-saving method for those who are not afraid of purchasing an extra pound or two of grain.

Avoiding a Stuck Sparge when All Grain Brewing

Before we jump into more advanced mashing techniques, it is important to mention a common problem that intermediate brewers often encounter: the stuck sparge.

A stuck sparge can be a painful experience when brewing all grain beers. New all grain brewers often find their sparge has come to a complete halt when brewing their favorite beer, so in this section we'll explore ways to avoid the stuck sparge.

The cause of a stuck sparge is quite simple – a stuck sparge occurs when your grain bed and filter mesh at the bottom of your lauter tun get completely clogged with bits of grain and no longer allow wort to flow. The flow of wort from the lauter tun into the brewing pot will slow to a trickle and then stop completely. While this problem occurs more often when using high protein adjuncts such as wheat malt, it can occur with almost any brew.

Avoiding the Stuck Sparge

The best thing to do about your stuck sparge is to avoid it in the first place. Here are some strategies for doing this:

- **Properly Mill your Grains:** The crush of your grains has a significant impact on your sparge as the grains form the filter bed needed for proper sparging. You can control the milling of your grains using an adjustable dual roller grain mill such as the Barley Crusher. An ideal milling with break the internal bits of grain into a coarse powder while still leaving the bulk of the husks intact. The husks then form the filter bed for your sparge. In general, dual roller mills do the best job overall. Adjust the gap on your mill to achieve as fine a crush as possible without destroying the hull integrity.
- **Use a Well Designed Mash Tun:** There are many systems home brewers use to act as a filter such as false bottoms,

stainless steel braid, and cut copper tubing. In general the filter area of the false bottom should be as broad as possible with the width and height of the filter area approximately equal to the depth of the grain bed. Cylindrical Gott or Igloo water coolers with a false bottom work very well. Whatever system you use, be sure you have a large area covered by the filter, with the filter elements evenly spaced across the bed. Poorly designed filters or false bottoms are prone to clogging.

- **Mash Out** - A mash out step is an extra infusion step that raises the temperature of the mash to approximately 168F (76 C), and halts the active enzymes used during the mash. More importantly, a mash out step raises the mash temperature making the sticky sugars in the wort more soluble, resulting in a slightly thinner and less sticky wort. The less sticky wort helps reduce the chance of a stuck mash.

- **Keep the Grain Bed Afloat** - If fly sparging or batch sparging, it is important to keep the grain bed afloat with a small layer of water above the grain bed. If you let the sparge water run too low, the top of the grain bed will dry out, compressing the entire grain bed and increasing the chance of a stuck mash. Adjust the flow of water into your lauter tun to keep a layer of water over the grain bed so the top of the grain bed is floating and not compressed.

- **Add Rice Hulls** - Rice hulls, available from most brewing stores, add no flavor or sugars to the beer but can significantly reduce the chance of a stuck mash by providing a proper grain bed that filters the wort. Rice hulls are particularly useful for recipes using high protein additives such as large amounts of wheat or flaked barley.

Dealing with a Stuck Mash

What should you do if you already have a stuck mash? Here are a few steps you can take if you are faced with this difficult situation already:

- **Float the Grains** – Unless you are at the very end of the sparge, add water to float the grains, which will help to expand the grain bed and free your stuck sparge.
- **Add Hot Sparge Water** - If the temperature of the grain bed is below 168F (76 C), you can add hot water to the grain bed to raise the overall temperature to 168F (76 C). This will help reduce the viscosity of your wort and aid in breaking the stuck sparge. However, make sure you don't raise the temperature above 170F (77 C) (overall), as this could result in extraction of unwanted tannins from the grains.
- **Stir the Grain Bed** – Though in general you always want to avoid disturbing the grain bed once it is set, you can stir up the grain bed as a last resort. This will almost always break the stuck sparge, but it also will result in some grain material being released into the wort and also hurt your overall efficiency. You can help mitigate both of these by drawing a few quarts of wort off the grain bed after stirring and recycling these back into the top of your lauter tun until the wort runs clear again.

Advanced Mashing

In our introduction to mashing, we introduced the single step infusion mash which uses a single mash step in the range of 148-158F (64-70C) to convert complex sugars in the barley grain to simple sugars that can be fermented. In this section, I'll cover some of the other enzymes active in a barley mash that may be used to design more complex mash schedules such as multi-step infusion and decoction mashes.

Mash Enzymes

Mashing relies on an array of naturally occurring enzymes in malted barley to break complex sugars chains into less complex ones. The process starts during malting when the barley grains are germinated and dried. Beta-glucanese and proteolytic enzymes start to divide branches of complex sugars into shorter chains.

During the mash, the heavy lifting is done by diastatic enzymes that break down the protein and carbohydrate chains that lock up fermentable sugars. Further, as these starches are heated they become more soluble in water, making it possible to extract the sugars and create the sweet wort extracted during lautering. Crushing the grain before mashing increases solubility, making it possible to extract a larger percentage of the sugars and starch.

Here's a summary of the major enzyme groups found naturally in malted barley and their active range. While this appears complex at first, in practice the ranges overlap making simple multi-step mash schedules possible.

- **Phytase** (86-126F or 30-52C) – Lowers the pH of the mash. Lowering the mash pH has a number of benefits, though modern brewers rarely use a Phytase rest.
- **Debranching** (95-112F or 35-44C) – Helps to increase the solubility of starches resulting in increased extraction for certain malts.
- **Beta Glucanese** (95-113F or 35-45C) – Breaks down the gummy heavy starches, which can help improve stability and extraction, particularly for mashes high in proteins and adjuncts such as wheat.
- **Pepidase** (113-131F or 45-55C) – Produces free amino nitrogen, which can aid in fermentation.
- **Beta Amylase** (131-150F or 55-66C) – Produces maltose, the main sugar fermented in beer.
- **Alpha Amylase** (154-162F or 68-72C) – Produces a variety of sugars, including maltose and also some unfermentable sugars. Mashing at the higher end of this range produces more unfermentables and therefore more body in the finished beer.

Mash Schedules and Mash Steps

For all mash schedules, the "main step" is called the conversion or saccharrification step. The alpha and beta amylase enzymes, both of which are active to some degree in the normal 148-158F (64-70C) conversion step range, do the bulk work of mashing during this step. All mash profiles use a conversion step in this range.

Within the normal conversion range of 148-158F (64-70C), you can mash at the lower end of the range 148-152F (64-67C) to activate more beta amylase, resulting in more maltose conversion. Maltose is the primary sugar preferred by yeast, so a lower mash temperature results in a larger percentage of sugars being fermented resulting in a clean beer finish. This gives higher attenuation, slightly higher alcohol content and less body overall. It does generally take a bit longer for beta amylase to do its work, so a longer conversion step at low temperature is needed.

Mashing at the high end of the conversion range of 154-158F (68-70C) activates alpha amylase, resulting in not only maltose but also some unfermentable sugars. Less of the sugars will ferment, leaving lower yeast attenuation and additional body in the finished beer. Alpha amylase completes its work more quickly than beta, so a slightly shorter mash step time can be used.

In addition to the conversion step, some mash profiles add a dough-in rest, also called a protein rest. The protein rest is done at a temperature between 100-120F (38-49C) and allows the grains to soak and saturate as well as allowing the key various lower temperature enzymes to begin chopping up longer chains of molecules. This will generally lower your pH slightly, and improve your mash efficiency by a few percent. I personally recommend a 20-minute dough-in at a temperature between 100-112F (38-44C) for maximum impact.

Another popular step in many mash profiles is a "mash-out" step. A mash-out is done not to activate enzymes but actually to deactivate them. The mash out step raises the temperature of the mash to 168F (75.6C) to stop the conversion being performed by alpha and beta amylase. It also aids in sparging as the hot wort flows more easily through the grain bed. You can add a mash-out step to any mash profile, so you will frequently see single and two step mashes either with or without mash-out steps.

Very few mash profiles use more than the two steps covered earlier (protein rest and conversion step) with the optional addition of a mash-out step. Those that do add additional steps either include an "acid rest" at around 95F (35C) to lower the pH of the wort or divide the conversion step into two steps, one at 148F (64.4C) and one at 158F (70C), which fully activates both the alpha and beta amylase enzymes to provide for full conversion.

The Brew in a Bag Mashing Method

Brew in a Bag (BIAB) all grain beer brewing is a recent method for all grain brewing that originated in Australia. BIAB is an inexpensive way to for homebrewers to transition to all grain or partial mash brewing with less equipment than traditional infusion methods. Brewers also enjoy brew in a bag methods for the shorter setup, brewing and cleanup times.

The concept behind "brew in a bag" is to move to all grain brewing with minimal extra equipment, setup or time. The BIAB method involves using a grain bag set in the brew pot to mash the grains, followed by a sparge step where the bag is removed from the pot and the remaining wort is boiled as you would any other beer. While less efficient than traditional methods, you can easily compensate for this by using a little more grain in the mash.

Brew in a Bag Equipment

For an all grain batch, you need a full size (batch size plus a few gallons) boil pot and ideally a propane burner to quickly boil it. For partial mash brewers, a smaller pot (3-4 gallons) (11-15 l) is acceptable as you will not be mashing or boiling the full size of your batch. The brew in a bag method eliminates the need for a mash tun, hot liquor pot, or lauter tun.

The only other equipment needed (aside from normal extract brewing equipment) is a large grain bag. The bag should be made of a mesh material and sewn together like a great pillowcase. It should be large enough to cover the entire inside of the boil pot, and have a drawstring or tie at the top to allow the bag to be closed.

The bag will line the boil pot and close to hold the grains during the mash. At the end of the mash the bag is slowly withdrawn along with the grains and the remaining wort is boiled, cooled and fermented as any beer would be.

The Brew in a Bag Method

Brew in a bag is usually done using a single step infusion mash; the same profile most all grain brewers use. This involves preheating the water in the mash tun to a predetermined temperature before adding the grains. In a major departure from traditional methods, the entire pre-boil volume of water is used for the mash.

In BeerSmith, you can do this by choosing a "single infusion, no mash out" mash profile and then setting the first mash step volume (choose details next to the mash profile, then double click on the first step) equal to your boil volume. You can also use the infusion tool to calculate initial strike additions, setting the strike volume equal to the initial boil volume for your batch. For a partial mash BIAB, less water is typically used – but again it is equal to your starting boil volume.

Once the strike water is heated to the appropriate starting temperature, the bag is added to line the edge of the boil pot, and the grains are added. Done correctly, you should come very close to your target temperature for mash conversion – usually between 148 and 158 F (64 and 70C).

Once you reach your target mash temperature, it is best to cover your pot and maintain the temperature as steady as possible for the next 30-60 minutes while the complex sugars in the grain are converted to simple ones. You can also wrap the pot in towels or a blanket to help maintain a constant temperature.

After the mash is complete you have the option of heating the mash slightly to a mash out temperature (around 168F/76C). If you are planning to heat the pot while the bag is still in it, you do need some kind of screen or false bottom at the bottom to prevent the bag from getting burned or melted by direct heat from the burner. For BIAB, the mash out aids overall extraction efficiency when you remove the bag.

Finally, slowly lift the grain bag out of the pot and let it drain. Once the bag has drained you can empty it, spray it down and clean it off for reuse on your next batch of beer.

From this point forward, the wort left in your boil pot can be boiled, cooled and fermented just as you would any batch of beer. If brewing all grain, simply boil the wort with hop additions, cool it and transfer to your fermenter. For partial mash, you can add your extract, hops and continue to brew.

Advantages and Disadvantages
Some of the advantages of the brew in a bag method include:

- **Equipment Cost** – If you have a large brew pot already, the only additional equipment needed is a bag, which you can make yourself if you have access to a sewing machine.

- **Simplicity** – Brew in a bag lets you move to all grain or partial mash brewing in a simple way, and the method itself is very easy to execute, even with limited space.

The limitations include:

- **Batch Size** – All of the grains have to fit in the bag, and the bag has to be lifted out without breaking, so this does place some limitations on high gravity batches. However with a properly stitched grain bag, double batches are possible though a pulley may be desirable.
- **Efficiency** - Since BIAB is a full volume method, you will lose a few percent efficiency – overall batch efficiency is usually lower than with fly sparge methods. However, this can easily be compensated by adding a little more grain to the batch and formulating your recipes with the appropriate lower brewhouse efficiency estimate. Experienced BIAB brewers have reported efficiency as high as 80% in some cases.
- **Maintaining Mash Temperature** – Unless you have an insulated boil pot it can be difficult to maintain an aluminum or stainless pot at a constant mash temperature for the entire mash. You can partially mitigate this using blankets or towels wrapped around the pot.
- **High Water to Grain Ratio** – Mashing at a high water to grain ratio, as is the case here, results in lower levels of beta-amylase, resulting in more dextrines in the finished beer. This can translate to higher body than desired at the high end of the mash temperature range (156-158F or 69-70C). Conversely, the thin mash also works poorly at the low end (148-150F or 64-65C), creating dry beer. In general BIAB works best in the mid mash temperature range (150-156F or 65-69C). Finally, if you are brewing a beer high in non-barley adjuncts such as flaked wheat, BIAB may not be the best option.

Overall, BIAB is growing in popularity with many all grain brewers due to its simplicity and the small amount of equipment needed. I think it provides a great alternative, particularly for those first starting with all grain or looking to simplify their brew day.

Decoction Mashing

At the other end of the spectrum from BIAB methods, is decoction mashing. Decoction mashing is a bit more complex and time consuming than BIAB or infusion mashing, but it offers some significant advantages for popular European beer styles.

Decoction mashing involves nothing more than extracting a fraction of your mash mixture and bringing that portion to a boil in a separate vessel. Then the boiling wort is added back to the original wort to raise the temperature of the entire mixture for the next mash step. So instead of adding hot water as we did with the infusion method, we "decoct" or remove and boil a portion of the wort, then add it back to raise the temperature of the wort. All that is required is a separate smaller pot and heat source.

History of Decoction Mashing

Decoction mashing, which originated in Europe, predates common use of the thermometer. In those early days, it was difficult to achieve accurate infusion temperatures for an infusion mash, and also malts were under-modified compared to the highly modified malt we have today, requiring multiple step mash profiles. Brewers discovered by trial and error that if they extracted a fixed fraction of the mash and boiled it they could achieve the accurate temperature steps needed to mash their malts.

Decoction was used extensively in continental European recipes, and is still heavily used in many German and Bohemian styles. Some commercial brewers today use decoction mashing as well because it results in higher efficiency rates and also maximum extraction of flavor from the malt.

Why use Decoction Mashing

The first thing most all grain brewers learn is that they should not overheat their mash or they will risk killing off the enzymes needed to convert sugars, effectively stopping conversion. Yet in a strange paradox, decoction mashing actually results in higher conversion rates than infusion mashing. In fact, decoction mashing has a number of benefits:

- Boiling extracts maximal flavor from the malt, which can be a real advantage for many malty styles of beer including German beer styles.
- Boiling the mash destroys the grain cell walls, releasing additional enzymes for conversion and resulting in a higher extract conversion rate than infusion mashing.
- Boiling wort will carmelize a portion of it, again enhancing the malty flavor of the beer.
- Proteins in the mash tend to coagulate during the boil and are filtered out during lauter resulting in better clarity.

At the same time, some care must be taken while using the decoction method. Decoction does take longer than a single infusion mash. When heating the decocted fraction, you need to monitor it carefully to avoid scorching the mash on the bottom of the pan. Safety is a concern when handling large quantities of hot wort, and you must be careful not to splash the wort to avoid hot side aeration.

The Decoction Method

All decoction mashes start with a single infusion step where hot water is added to the mash to start the mashing process. Typical temperatures for the first step vary. Multiple step decoctions are often used. Some examples of steps include:

- 95F (35C) – Acid and Glucanese rest – to break down gummy solids (glucose) and lower pH of the mash for undermodified malts
- 127F (52C) – Protein rest
- 145F-153F (63-67C) – Beta Amylase Rest (start of conversion)
- 158-167F (72-75C) – Alpha Amylase Rest (main conversion step)

Decoction mash profiles may have one, two or even three decoctions. When selecting a decoction profile, keep in mind that many of the traditional multi-step decoction methods were designed for undermodified malts as opposed to modern modified malts. Generally only one conversion step is needed for modern highly modified malts. However, multiple step decoction methods will add a unique character and flavor to your beer.

The amount of water used in a decoction can vary tremendously. Traditional infusion mashes and many modern decoction methods use a relatively thick ratio of 1.25-1.5 quarts per pound (2.6-3.1 l/kg) of grain. Older decoction mash profiles often used much higher water to grain ratios – as high as 2 or even 3 quarts per pound of grain (4.1-6.3 l/kg). Slightly higher conversion rates are possible at the lower ratios, but some purists still use the high traditional water-to-grain ratios to reduce the chance of scorching. You also need to consider what will fit in your mash tun and boil pot.

The initial strike water is calculated as if it was a normal infusion, and can be done using the BeerSmith strike temperature tool or an online calculator. Typically the first infusion targets either 95F/35C (an acid rest) or 127F/53C (a protein rest).

After the infusion step, a fraction of the mash is decocted (drawn) and put in a separate pot to be slowly heated to a boil.

Some people argue whether the thin part of the mash or thick part should be drawn. I generally try to get a representative sample of the mash, including both grains and wort.

Calculating the fraction of the mash to decoct can be easily done. A program like BeerSmith has a separate tool for calculating decoctions and an integrated mash profile system that provides step by step mashing instructions.

Alternately, a quick web search will provide you with online decoction calculators. If you prefer doing it by hand, you can calculate the following fraction:

Fraction = (step_temp – initial_temp) / (boil_temp – initial_temp – equip_factor)

Where Fraction is the fraction to decoct, step_temp is the target step temperature, initial_temp is the initial (current) temperature of the mash, boil_temp is the temperature of the boiling mash (usually slightly above 212F or 100C at sea level) and equip_factor is an equipment dependent parameter (typically 18F or 10C).

Care must be taken when boiling the mash to avoid scorching on the bottom of the pot. Mix the mash continuously and heat it gently. Once the decoction starts to boil you can add it back to the original mash and mix thoroughly to achieve the next step temperature. Hold each step for the recommended time, much as you would with any infusion mash and continue with additional decoctions or sparging.

Finally, if you are using a decoction to achieve mash out temperature (usually around 168F/76C target temperature), you need to draw only the liquid portion of the mash as mashing out with a large portion of grains for mash out can result in undesirable flavors.

The Importance of Brewing Water

We now switch from mashing to brewing water. Brewing water plays a large role in the flavor of your homebrewed beer. Knowing the character of your local water source as well as how to adjust it to improve your beer is a critical skill, particularly for more advanced brewers.

Water impacts beer in three ways. Water ions are critical in the mashing process for all grain brewers, where the character of the water determines the efficiency and flavor of the extracted wort. Water also affects the perceived bitterness and hop utilization of finished beer. Finally, water adds flavor directly to the beer itself – as water is the largest single component in finished beer.

The effect of brewing water on beer can be characterized by six main water ions: Carbonate, Sodium, Chloride, Sulfate, Calcium and Magnesium.

Historically, many famous beer styles came to exist due to the local water: acid rests, protein rests and decoction mashes helped extract more calcium from the husks in low-mineral Pilsen, where Bohemian Pilsener was born. Indeed, acid rests were original done to "acidify" the mash when calcium and magnesium were deficient. Today, with fully modified grains and understanding of water chemistry, acid rests are not needed.

You can get a water report from your local municipality that will contain the mineral content of your water supply. On a water report you will often see these listed as parts per million (ppm) which is equivalent to one milligram per liter (mg/l). Each of the critical ions is described below:

Carbonate and Bicarbonate (CO3 and HCO3)

Carbonate is considered the most important ion for all grain brewing. Carbonate (or bicarbonate), expressed as "total alkalinity" on many water reports, is the ion that determines the acidity of the mash. It also is the primary determinant in the level of "temporary hardness" of the water. If carbonate levels are too low, the mash will be too acidic, especially when using darker malts (which have higher acidity). If carbonate is too high, mash efficiency will suffer.

Recommended levels are 25-50 mg/l for pale beers and 100-300 mg/l for darker beers. Note that pre-boiling the water can reduce bicarbonates and temporary hardness – the precipitate that falls out after boiling is primarily bicarbonate.

Sodium (Na)

Sodium contributes body and mouthfeel to the beer, but if used in excess will result in salty seawater flavors. High sodium water often comes from household water softeners, which is why I recommend against mashing with softened water. Sodium levels in the 10-70 mg/l range are normal, and levels of up to 150 mg/l can enhance malty body and fullness, but levels above 200 mg/l are undesirable.

Chloride (Cl)

Chloride, like sodium, also enhances the mouthfeel and complexity of the beer in low concentrations. Chlorine (which contains chloride) is often used in city water supplies to sanitize, and can also reach high concentrations from the use of bleach as a brewing sanitizer. Heavily chlorinated water will result in mediciny or chlorine-like flavors that are undesirable in finished beer. Normal brewing levels should be below 150 mg/l and never exceed 200 mg/l. If you have heavily chlorinated city water you can reduce it using a carbon filter or by pre-boiling the water for 20-30 minutes before use.

Sulfate (SO4)

Sulfate plays a major role in bringing out hop bitterness and accentuates the dry, sharp, hoppy profile in well hopped beers. It also plays a secondary role to lowering Ph of the mash, but the effect is much less than with carbonates as sulfate is only weakly alkaline. High levels of sulfate will create an astringent profile that is not desirable. Normal levels are 10-50 mg/l for pilsners and light beers and 30-70mg for most ales. Levels from 100-130 mg/l are used in Vienna and Dortmunder styles to enhance bitterness, and Burton on Trent pale ales use concentrations as high as 500 mg/l.

Calcium (Ca)

Calcium is the primary ion determining the "permanent hardness" of the water. Calcium plays multiple roles in the brewing process including lowering the Ph during mashing, aiding in precipitation of proteins during the boil, enhancing beer stability and also acting as an important yeast nutrient. Calcium levels in the 100 mg/l range are highly desirable, and additives should be considered if your water profile has calcium levels below 50 mg/l. The range 50mg/l to 150 mg/l is preferred for brewing.

Magnesium (Mg)

Magnesium is a critical yeast nutrient if used in small amounts. It also behaves as calcium in contributing to water hardness, but this is a secondary role. Levels in the 10-30 mg/l range are desirable, primarily to aid yeast growth. Levels above 30 mg/l will give a dry, astringent or sour or bitter taste to the beer.

You can get a profile of your local water supply from your city or water company. Also, often the local brewing club has already collected local water profiles for you to examine. In the water report, look for the 6 critical items listed above. Also, be aware that many local water suppliers will flush their system for a few weeks (often in the Spring) with highly chlorinated water, which can give you some very strange brewing results if you are unaware of their schedule.

Adjusting your Water

Different styles of beer require different water profiles. Often a particular beer is associated with the water profile of the city in which the beer originated. For a listing of water profiles for popular brewing cities of the world, you can visit our water profile listing at **BeerSmith.com** on the support page.

You can dilute your local tap water with distilled water if some ion counts are too high for your target water profile. Similarly you can use additives to increase the level of key ions. Popular additives include table salt (NaCl), Gypsum (CaSO4), Calcium Chloride (CaCl), Epsom Salts (MgSO4), Baking Soda (NaHCO3), and Chalk (CaCO3).

Unfortunately the additives do not add a straightforward amount of ions to the water profile, so it's best to use some kind of water profile tool to adjust your local water supply to reach a target profile. Usually only a few grams of additives is required to achieve your target profile. BeerSmith has a water profile tool available to perform this very function. Other water profile tools are also available online.

Mash Water pH – A Secret for Great Brews

For many years I never worried about balancing pH or even what my water profile was when brewing. After all, the beer was fine and most of the time I was brewing with extract, so pH did not matter much.

However, once I started all grain brewing, the water I brewed with suddenly started to matter. In fact, most professional brewers will tell you that mash pH can make the difference between great beer and average beer.

I also moved to an area with extremely hard water, which forced me to use bottled water to produce anything reasonably resembling beer. It turns out that the pH of your mash has a huge impact on the mashing process as well as taste of your finished all-grain beer.

Understanding pH: Alkalinity and Acidity

PH measures the acidity of a liquid. Pure water has a pH of 7.0, which means that it is neither acidic nor alkaline. If you are into chemistry, this means that the free H+ (hydronium) ions are balanced with the OH- (hydroxide) ions giving equal concentrations capable of forming H2O. If water has an excess of H+ ions, we call it acidic (lower pH), while an excess of OH- ions gives us alkaline (higher pH) water.

Now it we take our pure water in the form of rain and run it down through the atmosphere and soil it picks up CO2 and Calcium from the soil, these elements will bind with the H+ ions leaving a bunch of free OH- (hydroxide) ions making our water more alkaline. This increases the pH of the water. Most tap water is slightly alkaline for this reason. Really hard water can be highly alkaline.

Interestingly all malts (and dark malts in particular) have phosphates in them that react with the calcium and magnesium ions in alkaline water freeing up H+ ions that make the mixture acidic. Adding malt, especially dark malt, lowers the pH of the malt-water mixture in the mash.

The Importance of Mash pH

The pH of the mash is very important for proper conversion of sugars during the mash and also due to its effect on finished beer. Mashing should always take place at a pH between 5.1 and 5.3. However, it's important to note that we are talking about the pH of the mixed mash, which as I point out above depends on the color and quantity of malts added to the beer. For most light color beers, the mixed mash will be slightly alkaline (pH above 5.3) and require an acidic addition or buffer to bring it down to 5.2. Darker beers may already be near 5.2 pH as dark barley malts are more acidic.

Though some commercial brewers can accurately predict the pH of their mash in advance, few homebrewers have the detailed grain or water knowledge available to do this. The problem is that the color, quantity and even type and supplier of the malt can change the pH. In addition, your starting water and its interactions with the malts may vary with each recipe. Remember that commercial brewers brew the same recipe every time using the same ingredients, while homebrewers do this only rarely.

That's why homebrewers are reduced to measuring the pH of each mash right after it is mixed and then adjusting our pH as early as possible in the mashing process.

Measuring pH can be done in several ways including pH (litmus) strips, precison pH strips and even using an electronic pH meter. A pH strip is a small strip of paper you use with a color chart to measure the pH of your wort. Of the three methods, precision pH strips are usually most cost effective and practical. Standard pH strips lack the precision needed to measure down to a tenth of a point pH, and electronic meters are expensive and require frequent replacement of the electrodes to maintain accuracy.

Another practical consideration is that the mash is usually hot, so you need to adjust the pH reading for temperature. Hot wort will almost always provide a higher pH reading than the actual wort. You can compensate for this either by rapidly cooling the sample to room temperature before measuring or applying a correction factor after taking the reading. Check the documentation with your pH strips to determine the appropriate correction.

Methods for Adjusting Mash pH
There are several methods available to the homebrewer for adjusting the pH of your wort. As noted earlier, in most cases you will need to lower your pH to reach the 5.2 target level.

- **Calcium and Magnesium Salts:** Three salts, Gypsum (CaSO4), Epsom Salt (MgSO4) and Calcium Chloride (CaCl) can be added to lower your pH. The calcium and magnesium ions in these additions reduce the alkalinity of the water. Note, however, that the sulfate and chloride ions react with the phosphates from the mash, which can lead to undesirable flavors. As a result you need to limit the amount added. You can calculate appropriate amounts using a water tool such as the one in BeerSmith. Suggested limits are 50-150 ppm for calcium, 50-150 ppm for sulfate, 0-150 ppm for chloride and 10-30 ppm for magnesium.

- **Food Grade Acids -** Acid additions counter the H+ ion and directly lower the alkalinity of the mash. Popular additions include phosphoric acid, sulfuric acid and lactic acid. All of these contribute other flavors and ions to the beer as well, which can again cause problems if used in excessive amounts. Phosphoric acid is used to make soda, and will contribute phosphates to the mash. Lactic acid will add lactates, which are used in many Belgian styles to sour the beer. Sulfuric acid will contribute sulfates. In general you should add the minimum needed to achieve your target pH. The amount will vary depending on the concentration of your acid and wort volume.

- **Acid Malt** – Because of German purity laws (the Reinheitsgebot) that prevent additives to German beer, sour malt (called acid malt) is used to aid in the brewing of light beers to lower mash pH. Acid malt is made by souring malt with lactic bacteria for a short period which effectively creates lactic acid. Adding acid malt is effectively equivalent to adding lactic acid to the mash. Adding one percent of acid malt effectively lowers the pH of the malt by approximately 0.1 pH.

- **Sour Mash -** Another technique developed by the Germans is to create a sour mash, which again contains lactic acid produced by lactic bacteria. The technique is to mash a quantity of grain, cools it to about 80F and then adds some fresh malt (which contains lots of lactic bacteria naturally) and let the mixture sit overnight. The bacteria will quickly sour the mash and start fermenting it, again creating lactic acid. The next day this sour mash can be mixed with a regular mash to lower its pH. The challenge with sour mashing is that it can be somewhat inconsistent in pH and also labor intensive.

- **Acid Rest** - Though seldom used today thanks to modern highly modified malts, an acid rest in the 95F (35C) range can break down phytins in the malt into phytic acid that will lower the mash pH. This was traditionally done in German triple decoction mashes, and is most effective when used with undermodified malts.
- **5.2 Stabilizer** – A number of brew stores now carry an additive called 5.2 stabilizer. This is a powder you can add to the beer to lower the mash pH to 5.2. It consists of buffers that reduce the alkalinity of the mash to reach a 5.2 level. As long as your starting water is not completely out of kilter, this is a good simple solution for many homebrewers.

If you want to brew world class all grain or partial mash beers, you need to measure and adjust your mash pH. It has a huge impact on the quality of your finished beer.

Conditioned and Wet Grain Milling

Have you ever had a problem with finely crushed malt creating a stuck sparge when home brewing? In this section we look at how wet and conditioned milling can help reduce the chance of a stuck sparge by creating a more porus grain bed. While I would not call this a mainstream technique, it is an interesting path to explore for the more advanced all grain brewer.

Why Wet Mill?

I knew little about wet milling or its variants until a recent article (Mar-Apr 2010, *Brew Your Own Magazine*) highlighted the technique. While rarely used in the US, this technique attempts to raise the moisture content of the grain by 20-30% using steam or a hot spray of water.

The wet grain is then run through your malt mill at a narrower than usual gap to split the interior from the grain husk. Done properly, you will get larger segments of intact grain husk. The advantage is a more porus grain bed without the dusty grain particles produced by dry milling. This can make a stuck sparge less likely.

Conditioned Milling

I do not recommend trying this unless you have a two roller grain mill such as the Barley Crusher, as other types of grain mills could get gummed up by the wet grains. Even then, one must be careful not to overexpose the grains, as grains that are too wet will gum up the mill.

Pure wet milling is difficult to duplicate in a home environment, but two practical conditioned milling options exist for the homebrewer. One is to use a short exposure to steam, while the second method requires spraying with hot water for a short period of time.

The steam options requires a large pot of boiling water and a false bottom. Put the grains in a large grain bag and set it aside. Then bring the pot to a boil. Once you had a strong boil going, place the bag over the steam rising from it for about a minute and a half. Then pull the bag out of the steam, stir it a bit and quickly mill it.

A second option, described in the BYO article, involves sprinkling hot water at 158F/70C over the grains. Here it is best to treat a smaller amount of grain at a time over a lauter tun or false bottom, so the spray can reach all of the grains. Heat water to 158F and put it in a spray bottle or watering can, and lightly spray the grains for 60 seconds, allowing excess water to drop off. Allow the malt to sit for a minute or two to absorb as much water as possible and then mill it. Reportedly this technique results in slightly higher water content than steaming.

Milling the Grains

The milling itself should be straightforward, but start as quickly as possible. Set the malt mill at a slightly narrower gap than normal, and proceed to mill. If the mill starts to get gummed up with wet grain, then stop as you have probably gone too far with the water. You want the husks to come out slightly wet and intact, but the inside of the grains to be largely dry. If too wet, let the grains dry for a bit before proceeding.

If you compare some dry milled malt to the conditioned malt you should see a marked difference particularly in the larger pieces of husk and reduced amount of grain dust. I will note that this is not a technique you should need for every batch. A properly set malt mill should produce a great dry mill crush and normal sparge for most beers. However, if you are brewing a beer with a lot of sticky adjuncts such as wheats, unmalted barley, and like to experiment, then give it a try.

Run some dry malt through your mill at the end to help clean up any mess you have left, and then dry the entire mill. It's best not to leave gobs of wet malt sitting on your steel rollers.

Diastatic Power and Mashing

While rarely covered in other home brewing books, diastatic power is an important concept, especially for home brewers making beers with high percentages of non-barley or specialty grains. Partial mash brewers must also pay attention to diastatic power since they are often mashing with a high percentage of specialty grains.

The Malting Process

The story of diastatic power starts as part of the malting process. As you will see in an upcoming section on "Malting at Home" the malting process consists of placing raw barley grains in water and germinating (sprouting or growing) them until the acrospire (the little leaf growing inside the husk) reaches a length close to that of the grain itself. The malt is then kiln dried, and the tiny sproutlets fall off, leaving malted barley. For darker and specialty grains the malt is roasted at varying degrees of time and temperature to achieve everything from caramel malt to stout roast.

The purpose of the malting process is primarily to break down the protein structure of the hard grains and make them friable for mashing. In fact, you may often hear the term "modification" of the malt. Highly modified malt has almost all of its protein structure broken down, while undermodified malt still contains a significant portion of unfermentable proteins and complex starches. A secondary effect of malting, however, is to develop the enzymes (notably beta amylase) needed for mashing.

Diastatic Power

Diastatic power refers to the enzymatic power of the malt itself – its ability to break down starches into even simpler fermentable sugars during the mashing process. The term "diastatic" refers to "diastase" enzymes. There are two "diastase" enzymes, the first is alpha amylase and the second is beta amylase. These enzymes might be familiar to many of you who have been brewing all grain for a while, as they are the primary enzymes active when you mash your grains in the normal temperature range of 148-158F (64-70C).

So why should an average home brewer care? If you don't have sufficient diastatic enzymes in your mash, you simply will not be able to properly convert sugars during the mash. This will leave you with a partially fermented very sweet beer, with low alcohol content.

Diastatic Power is measured in degrees lintner (often denoted with a big °L), though in Europe a secondary measure of Windisch-Kolbach units (degrees °WK) is often used. You can convert from one to the other using Lintner=(WK+16)/3.5 or going the other way as WK=3.5*Lintner − 16. A malt needs a diastatic power of approximately 35 °L to be considered "self converting". Some of the newest American 6-row malts can have a diastatic power as high as 160 °L.

You can get the lintner values for many common types of malt from the malt supplier's specification sheet, or from our BeerSmith database. Let's look at sample lintner values for a few commonly used grains:

- American 2 Row Pale Malt: 140 °L
- American 6 Row Pale Malt: 160 °L
- British Pale Malts: 40-70 °L
- Maris Otter Pale Malt: 120 °L
- Belgian Pale Malt (2 row): 60 °L
- German Pilsner Malt: 110 °L
- Munich Malt (10 SRM): 70 °L
- Munich Malt (20 SRM): 25 °L
- Vienna Malt: 50 °L
- Wheat Malt, German: 60-90 °L
- Wheat, Unmalted (flaked, Torrified): 0 °L
- Crystal Malt (all): 0 °L
- Chocolate Malt: 0°L
- Black Patent Malts: 0 °L

A few things become obvious looking at the above examples. With the possible exception of the very lightest specialty base malts such as Vienna or Munich, few specialty malts provide very much enzymatic power. Almost all of the enzymes needed to convert your mash are contained in your base malt, so the selection of a good base malt is important. Wheat provides diastatic power nearly equal to barley so it can be used in large proportions to make wheat beer.

Diastatic Power for All Grain and Partial Mash Brewers
How does this affect your all grain brewing? Clearly if you are brewing an all grain batch with a high power base malt like American six row, you will have plenty of enzymes available to convert your mash, and it will also convert at a faster pace than it might otherwise. However, if you are using a low power 2-row British malt with a large number of specialty malts, the sugars will still convert but might take substantially longer to do so.

A few specific styles can also cause problems for the all grain brewer. Let's take the example of Belgian Wit, which typically is made from 60% pale malt and 40% unmalted wheat (often flaked or torrified). If you select a Belgian Pale Malt base malt with low diastatic power, you may be in for a very long mash as the unmalted wheat contributes no enzymes to the process. The grains will likely still convert (little of the unmalted wheat will convert in any case) but it may take a long time to reach full conversion.

Diastatic power plays an even more important role for partial mash brewers. Many beginning partial mash brewers tend to take several pounds of specialty malts and try to mash them without a pale base malt. This can cause very poor conversion, as the specialty malts lack the enzymes to convert. It is important that you mash with sufficient base malt to provide the enzymes needed in the mashing process.

Estimating Diastatic Power for your Mash
To get a quick idea of whether you have sufficient diastatic power in your all grain or partial mash brew, I recommend you simply average the weighted diastatic power of your

ingredients and see whether the final number is greater than the 30 Lintner minimum needed to convert. The overall diastatic power for your mash would be the sum of the diastatic power for each ingredient times its weight divided by the total grain weight. To get this number, just multiply the diastatic power for each grain times the weight of that grain, add the numbers up for all of your grains, and divide by the total grain weight.

Lintner_for_batch = Σ(lintner_for_grain * weight_of_grain) / (total_batch_grain_weight)

Let's look at a quick example: a partial mash using 2 lb (0.91 kg) of Caramel Malt, 1 pound (0.45 kg)of chocolate malt, and 1 pound (0.45 kg) of British Pale malt, with a diastatic power of 50 Lintner. The Caramel and Chocolate malts both have a diastatic power of zero, so they each contribute (0L x 1lbs) and (0L x 2lbs) for a total contribution of zero lintner-pounds. The pale malt is (50L x 1 lb) for a total contribution of 50 L-lbs. Now we add the contributions for all three up (which is 0+0+50) or 50 L-lbs.

Now we divide by the total grain weight in the mash which is simply 4 lbs, which leaves an overall average diastatic power of 50/4 or 12.5 Lintner. Since this number is smaller than the 30 lintner needed to convert the overall mash, another pound of pale malt or one with higher diastatic power might be warranted. The calculation would be the same in metric, except you would use weights in kilograms.

The above calculation is a rough approximation, as the specialty grains are only partially fermentable and contain many non-convertible starches, but I usually prefer to err on the side of more enzymes rather than end up short in the mash. Also, I don't like to wait forever for my mash to complete, so I will often shoot for a number higher than the 30 L limit shown above. Note that this calculation is really only needed for partial or full mashes with high percentages of specialty malts, as most modern pale base malts have very high diastatic power.

Chapter 7: Additional Brewing Techniques

"Without question, the greatest invention in the history of mankind is beer. Oh, I grant you that the wheel is also a fine invention, but the wheel does not go nearly as well with pizza." – Dave Berry

In this chapter we introduce a number of additional brewing techniques you can use to enhance your beer, make brewing easier or for special beer styles. As you gain more experience you will find that these techniques can help to improve your quality or expand your brewing horizons.

Yeast Washing: Reusing your Yeast

Washing yeast to reuse it in another batch of beer is a great technique to have in your home brewing arsenal. Yeast washing is a simple process used to separate the live yeast from the underlying trub (hops and spent grains) left at the bottom of your fermenter when making beer.

With the high price of ingredients, yeast washing is a great way to save a few dollars and also build a strong yeast culture as a basis for a yeast starter. Rather than purchase new yeast each time you can wash and reuse your yeast across as many as 5-6 batches spread out over a period of months by reusing yeast from your primary fermentation.

Yeast washing is remarkably easy to do, involves minimal equipment, and can be done in a short period of time. All that is required are two sanitized mason jars; some distilled or pre-boiled sanitized water and some plastic or foil to put over the jars. Sanitizing or sterilizing everything involved is critically important as yeast is susceptible to infection.

Washing your Yeast

Start by sterilizing your two high temperature mason jars by boiling them in water or immersing them in a high quality sanitizing solution. Prepare a few quarts of sterile water by pre-boiling it and then cooling it to room temperature. Use sanitizing solution such as iodophor to sanitize the rim of your fermenter.

If possible, you want to draw your yeast sample from the primary fermenter as it contains more active yeast than the secondary. Harvest the yeast immediately after racking your beer off to the secondary to minimize the chance of contamination. The primary will contain a layer of thick trub (sediment). You need a bit of liquid to work with, so add a quart of sterile water to the primary if needed.

Swish the fermenter around several times to break up the trub and then allow it to settle for a few minutes. Pour the liquid from the top of the trub into one of your mason jars, being careful to keep everything as sterile as possible.

After collecting your yeast and trub put some foil or plastic wrap over the top and seal it with a rubber band. Put the Mason jar in your refrigerator for 30-60 minutes, which will help it separate. Ideally you will see a clear separation between the liquid and sediment. The liquid contains suspended yeast, while the sediment is primarily trub.

The next step is simply to pour off the liquid suspended yeast from the top of your Mason jar leaving as much of the sediment behind as possible. Pour your yeast into a second mason jar, cover it and place it in the fridge again for storage.

Storage and Reuse

If you still have a significant amount of trub at the bottom of the second Mason jar, you may want to consider mixing in some sterile water and washing the yeast again. If not, you can store the yeast for several months in the refrigerator until you are ready to brew again. If you plan to store it for an extended period you may want to consider transferring it to a flask or bottle with an airlock and keep it in the refrigerator to prevent contamination.

On the day before you brew, add some wort to your yeast to create an appropriately sized yeast starter (see chapter 2) for your next batch. If you want to use your yeast across several batches you can either split your starter and store part of it for later use or repeat the entire process to collect yeast from the primary again.

If you do collect yeast across several generations, I recommend not exceeding 4-6 generations of reuse as eventually some wild yeasts or bacteria will make their way into your yeast.

Washing your yeast is a great way to save a few dollars while keeping a healthy supply of fresh yeast available for your favorite brew.

Brewing Beer with Honey

Honey, the main ingredient in mead, has become a popular addition for many beer brewers. Brewing with honey provides a rich array of aromas and flavors that add complexity and character to your beer. Here we'll take a look at some of the ways to incorporate honey into your home brewed beer.

I started brewing with honey some 24 years ago, in one of my very first batches of beer. To be fair, my knowledge level was low at that time, so I dumped the honey directly into the boil, then rapidly fermented and bottled it. This caused significant problems, as boiling the honey effectively boiled off much of the flavor and aroma, and the honey was not fully fermented resulting in significant instability and gushing bottles.

About Honey

Honey is a very complex ingredient. It contains a range of sugars, many simple and some complex as well as a plethora of living organisms including yeast, enzymes, and bacteria. It also has a very rich flavor profile with exotic, but fragile aromas. Unfortunately, boiling honey effectively boils off the delicate aromas and also deactivates many of the enzymes needed to break down and ferment the honey. Approximately 90-95% of the sugars in honey are fermentable.

This leaves a dilemma for the brewer, as you need to sterilize the honey to eliminate the bacteria without boiling off the aroma oils and destroying the enzymes.

Using Honey in Beer

The proper way to use honey with your beer is to pasteurize it without boiling it:

- Mix the honey with water to dilute it to approximately the same gravity as the wort you are planning to add it to.
- Heat the honey to approximately 176 F (80 C) and hold it for 60-90 minutes. Ideally you would like to keep the honey under a CO_2 blanket if you have a CO_2 tank, but if not at least cover the pot.
- After cooling the honey, add it directly to the beer while it is fermenting. Ideally it should be added at high kraeusen (when fermentation is at its maximum activity).
- Allow additional time to ferment before bottling. Honey takes a notoriously long time to fully ferment. At a minimum I would allow 3-8 weeks more for full fermentation, though many meads are fermented for a year or more.

The variety of honey to use depends on your desired flavor profile. Often the types used with mead are best, depending on the style of beer you are brewing and desired character.

The percentage of honey to use should be between approximately 2-10%. Adding too much honey will not only increase the needed fermentation time, but also give the beer a decidedly mead-like character. Personally, I recommend somewhere between 5-10% to give the beer a notable honey flavor and aroma without being overbearing.

Brewing Fruit Beers

Brewing fruit beer is not for everyone, but a properly balanced fruit beer can be light and refreshing on a hot summer day. Beers that include fruit vary widely in taste, style and strength. Whatever the style, a properly balanced fruit beer should not betray the underlying beer - fruit beer is beer with a touch of fruit flavor and not a wine cooler!

History

According to Randy Mosher's Radical Brewing book, fruit beer is a relatively modern invention of the 20th century. He notes that ancient Egyptians referred to the use of dates and pomegranates, but only a few passing references can be found for fruit in intervening years until the 1930's. Many of the most famous Belgian fruit beers like Kriek started at that time, with Framboise to follow 20 years later.

Fruit beers, like many styles, have enjoyed a resurgence with the microbrewery explosion the last 20 years in the United States. Wheat based fruit beers, in particular, have become popular enough to even be adopted by major US breweries.

Many of these beers contain no actual fruit. Instead they brew a light wheat beer or lager and add artificial fruit flavorings to provide a touch of fruit. Home brewers can do the same thing by purchasing artificial fruit flavor from a homebrew supply shop and adding an appropriate amount to their beers. Some commercial brews also use fruit extract. This works well for fruits like raspberry and apricots that maintain their flavor after fermentation.

Fruit to Use in Beer

Some fruits fair much better in beer than others. Fruits like uncooked blueberry and peach tend to lose much of their flavor when used in beer. Others like apricot and raspberry hold up well. Cherries fare well but often require extensive aging.

Here are a few popular fruits to consider for fruit beer:

- **Cherries** - Traditionally used in many Belgian beers. Ripe, sour cherries are best as they blend well with the malt flavors. Generally a lot of cherry is needed, as much as 2-4 lbs per gallon of beer, which is why many cherry based Belgian beers are expensive. Also, cherry beers need extensive aging.
- **Peaches** - Peach is one fruit that fades when used in beer. Apricot is a good substitute that creates a flavor similar to peach in the finished beer. Peach flavoring is also a possibility if you are determined to have peach.
- **Blueberry** - Another fruit that does not hold up well in beer. Some brewers claim that cooked blueberry holds up better than uncooked.
- **Raspberry** - Raspberry is one of the best fruits to use with beer. The flavor and aroma hold up well to fermentation, and come through well in the finished beer. The flavor is strong even at a rate of 0.5-1 lb per gallon, making raspberry a favorite of commercial beer brewers.
- **Blackberry** - Blackberry, like raspberry, is another great fruit to use in beer. However, they do not come through as intensely as raspberry, requiring a larger usage rate of 1-3+ pounds per gallon. The color also carries over well to the finished beer.

- **Strawberries** - Strawberry is generally a poor choice. The flavor, aroma and color fade quickly. If you are going to use strawberry you need fully ripe berries, must use a lot of them (2-5 lb per gallon) and you must drink the beer as young as possible as the flavor and aroma will be gone before you know it.
- **Apricots** - Much better than peaches, but produce a peach like flavor in the finished beer. If you want peach flavor, use apricots at a rate of 1.5-4 pounds per gallon. Apricot extract also produces good results.
- **Apples** - Produce only a mild flavoring. Generally apples are best used with meads and hard cider as they tend to be acidic in flavor.
- **Other Fruits** - A variety of other fruits are less commonly used in beers and meads to include pears, dates, bananas, plums, mangos, pomegranate, etc... Most of these fruits produce only a mild flavor and aroma, though they add considerable fermentable sugars. Some brewers report success with passion fruit and mangos, which both have strong aroma and flavor.

Brewing Beer with Fruit

Brewing beer with fruit involves a little bit of art and a bit of science. Fruit beers are generally formulated to be light tasting, light bodied, and also lightly hopped. The reason for this is simple - most fruits lose a lot of their flavor during fermentation, and a strong malt or hops flavor will tent to overpower the subtle fruit flavors, making the fruit undetectable in the finished beer. A lightly hopped wheat beer as the base beer is often a good choice, though properly balanced cherries or raspberries can sometimes come through in maltier beers.

For yeast, I've had the greatest success with clean finishing, high attenuation yeasts. This is not to say you could not try a more complex yeast, but low flocculation, low attenuation yeasts generally take longer to fully ferment the complex sugars in the fruit, and the complex flavors of the yeast don't always complement the fruit flavor itself. Also, the low flocculation yeasts create more clarity problems - which is already an issue with most fruit beers.

Another factor to consider when brewing with fruit is that most fruits have a substantial portion of fermentable sugar in them. If you are adding 1-3 lbs of fruit per gallon, this will have a substantial effect on the alcohol content of the finished beer. If you make a high gravity base beer to start, then add the fruit you will have a highly alcoholic beer (too much warmth) that can easily become unbalanced. You need to take into account the specific gravity added by the fruit as well as malts, then hop appropriately to achieve the proper balance between bitterness and sweetness.

Freeze whole fruit once and thaw it before adding it to the beer. Freezing fruit breaks open the cell walls, allowing more flavor and aroma to permeate the beer. Thaw it before use, however, to avoid shocking the yeast in your beer with a sudden change of temperature.

Add the fruit to the secondary fermenter if at all possible. Since whole fruit in particular contains a lot of microbes and bacteria, adding fruit too early in the fermentation process can lead to infection. By the time your beer is in the secondary fermenter, it has a higher alcoholic content, is more acidic and also nutrient depleted but yeast rich, all of which serve as a guard against potential infection.

One cautionary note when working with glass carboys as secondaries - adding fruit to your beer will cause rapid and vigorous fermentation, which requires several gallons of headspace above the beer. If you are fermenting in a closed container such as a carboy, be sure you have adequate headspace and ventilation to prevent the bubbling trub from blocking your airlock, which could make a bomb out of your glass carboy.

Juices and concentrates can also be used much like you would use the whole fruit - adding them to the secondary. Adjustments must be made for concentration however - obviously concentrated fruit juice contains more flavor/fermentables than thinned juice.

Fruit flavorings or artificial flavor additives contain no fermentable sugars, so these may be added directly to the beer just before bottling. In general, artificial fruit flavors are great at providing a burst of fruity flavor with minimum fuss but also produce a somewhat flat narrow flavor profile compared to real fruit. One advantage of artificial flavor extracts is that you can flavor to taste when bottling by adding a little extract at a time and then tasting the beer to meet your needs.

Beer clarity can be a significant problem when brewing with fruits. Most fruits contain pectins, carbohydrates and proteins that contribute to haze or cloudiness in the finished beer. I recommend the use of some kind of fining agent when brewing with fruit, and best results may be achieved if you use a combination of methods to achieve better clarity.

Aging is another issue that one must deal with when working with fruit beers. Fruits contain many complex sugars that frequently ferment out over a long timeframe. For bottle conditioned beers this can be a significant problem for the bottle that was perfectly carbonated a month or two after bottling may be an overcarbonated gusher a month or two later. Obviously kegging fruit beer avoids this problem.

The second aging issue is that the flavor profile of fruit beer will inevitably change over time as these complex sugars ferment. Young fruit beers may have a poor flavor profile due to unfermentables as well as the pectins, proteins and other complex fruit materials in the beer. At some point the flavor of the beer will definitely peak, but for some fruit beers this can take six months to even a year or more. One must be patient with fruit beer. Finally, as the fruit continues to change you may see a dropoff in quality once the beer is past its peak.

Brewing with fruit is a complex, challenging task that is not for the weak at heart! However a properly balanced fruit beer can be a refreshing reward for the adventurous brewer.

Soured Beer in Homebrewing

The use of soured beer is an ancient technique used to add character to many beer styles. One of my personal favorites, the Irish Stout, often includes a small addition of soured wort. Sour beer dates back to the ancient times, as the discovery of beer likely occurred when someone left some wet grains out and they started fermenting.

Souring is widely used in Belgian beers, where in many cases entire batches are left to sour in open vats, producing many sour styles such as Lambic and Flanders. Flanders brown is often made with blended sour and unsoured beer. I won't cover Lambics in great detail here, as the methods used for Lambics vary considerably, but also often include blending soured wort with unsoured beer.

Brewing with sour beer at home involves taking a portion of the wort from your mash (or for extract brewers, a portion from the boil) and setting it aside and either adding souring yeasts such as Lactobacillus or letting it sour naturally. Personally, I recommend getting some Lactobacillus culture such as Wyeast Labs #4335 "Lactobacillus Delbrueckii" as natural yeasts and bacteria can often go awry. For Lambics, Wyeast #3112 "Brettanomyces Bruxellensis" or Brewtek's "Brettanomyces Lambicus" are often used with other yeasts as part of the main fermentation or part of the fermentation. The spoiled wort is then pasteurized by heating it and added back into the original beer to give a slightly sour character to the beer. This will add character and a lactic sourness to the beer, which is desirable for many styles.

The Sour Wort Method

If you are brewing an all grain batch, a portion of the runnings from your mash tun should be collected and set aside in a separate container. For something like an Irish Stout, I typically would set aside 1/2 a quart of wort from the middle runnings of the mash and set it aside for a 5 gallon batch. A good rule of thumb is that your spoiled wort should only make up about 3-4% of your total finished volume for stouts, and up to 25% of your volume for a Flanders Brown Ale, though I recommend starting with less and blending to taste. If you use too much you will end up with excessively sour beer.

For extract brewers, you can draw a portion of the wort near the beginning of the boil, ideally after you add your extract but before adding the hops, as hops themselves can have an antibiotic effect.

Once you have collected your wort, set it aside in a small closed container and continue to brew the remainder of your batch in the normal way. For the sour portion I prefer to add a small amount of Lactobacillus bacteria strain to the wort, apply an airlock, and let it sour in a cool, dark location.

The soured wort will quickly get a sour smell, and likely a disgusting film over the top. After a few days it should be thoroughly infested and largely fermented. At this point, carefully siphon or skim and pour the liquid, attempting to leave as much of the scum and sediment behind as possible.

Pasteurizing and Use of Soured Beer

Place the soured wort in a pan and heat it to 170F and hold it there for at least 30 minutes. This will pasteurize the soured wort to kill off the bacteria and yeast without destroying the sour lactic acid flavor you want in your beer.

Rapidly cool the sour portion, being careful to handle it with sterilized equipment. Siphon or very gently pour the soured wort into your already fermenting main batch, and continue fermenting, aging and bottling the beer as you normally would.

Done properly, the sour wort method will produce a slight, but not overly pronounced sour edge to your beer. In styles such as classic Irish Stout, the sourness helps to enhance the overall flavor mix of stout roast barley and English hops. For Flanders, this provides the classic sour twang. This technique can also be used to sour some more sophisticated Belgian styles, though brewing a complex beast like a Lambic is beyond the scope of this particular chapter.

Krausening Beer

Krausening is a traditional German method for carbonating beers without using sugars or other adjuncts. Instead actively fermenting malt wort is added to the fermented beer to provide the malted sugars needed for carbonation.

The History of Krausening

The "Reinheitsgebot", or German purity law, originated in Bavaria in 1516. It specifies that beer may only be made from the three basic ingredients: malt, hops, and water. Interestingly, yeast was left out of the original law as it was unknown until Louis Pasteur discovered microorganisms in the late 1800's. It was recently replaced by the "Biergesetz" in 1993, which also allows the use of malted wheat and cane sugar, though the term "Reinheitsgebot" is more commonly used.

Since sugars were not allowed in beer, malt wort was used instead. Krausening was widely used in Germany particularly for lagers. Many lagers are cold fermented and aged, often causing the yeast to go dormant. By adding actively fermenting wort for carbonation the lager could be properly carbonated. Krausening was less commonly used in Kolsch or

Alt, as these ales were fermented at warmer temperatures leaving active yeast.

Krausening

In a brewery, krausening would be done with fresh wort taken from the most recent batch made. For the homebrewer, Krausening is most often done with a small amount of wort made from dry malt extract. Alternately you can use a fresh batch of wort or keep some wort in a sterile container in the refrigerator from your last batch.

A key question is how much wort to use for proper carbonation? A good rule of thumb is that you should add enough wort to raise the gravity of the beer three points. For simplicty you can try the following formula:

Quarts_of_wort = (12 x Gallons_of_beer) / ((Specific_gravity_wort – 1.0) * 1000)

For example, if the krausening addition of wort (also called gyle) has a specific gravity of 1.060, and we're krausening 5 gallons of beer, the result would be (12 x 5)/((1.060-1)*1000) which works out to exactly one quart of wort to add at bottling.

Traditionally, the krausening addition is added to the fermenter when the addition is at its most active point of fermentation. Ideally you should add yeast to your krausen and monitor it for active fermentation, but try to catch it before a lot of the malt sugars have been consumed. You need to measure the specific gravity of the krausening addition and do the above calculation before adding it to the wort to get the appropriate amount.

After you add the krausening wort, you can bottle or keg your beer and naturally carbonate it just as you would if you were using sugar to carbonate. Store your beer in a cool, dark place for a week or two to allow it to carbonate and then lager or age as desired.

Kegging your Home Brewed Beer

We now move from krausening to kegging. Would you like to learn how to start kegging your own beer? Kegging your homebrew saves time and offers a very convenient way to serve your beer. Kegging also offers a "cool factor" for friends who sample your beer. This section will walk you through the basics of purchasing a kegging system, filling your kegs and serving your kegged beer at home.

Purchase a Beer Kegging System

If you don't already have a beer kegging system, you can purchase one from your local homebrew store or a major online brewing supply store. A kegging system consists of a keg, a CO_2 (carbon dioxide) gas tank, a pressure regulator and two hoses. One hose feeds CO_2 gas into your keg inlet, and the other hose brings the beer from the keg to your tap. Keg sizes vary, but the most popular size is the 5 gallon Cornelius or "Corney" keg.

If you are just starting out with kegging your own beer, it is best to purchase a complete starter system from a single store. Complete systems typically run less than $200 for an initial setup including all of the supplies mentioned above. Several popular brewing supply stores that sell kegging equipment can be found on our web site. Once you have your kegging system you will need to fill the CO_2 tank with CO_2 from a local beverage supply or gas supply store.

In addition to the keg and tank, you need a regulator to adjust the pressure for your kegging system. I recommend you purchase a regulator with two dials on it. One will show the pressure inside the CO_2 tank, while the second one will show the pressure output to your keg line. Most regulators have a screw or knob to adjust the output pressure, and many also have a valve to shut off the CO_2 line out. As a safety precaution you should place the CO_2 tank in a container or tie it in a standing position so it cannot fall over and break off the regulator. A broken regulator or valve could turn the high pressure CO2 tank into a missile.

Before you carbonate and use your first keg, it is important to test your entire system for leaks. Apply some CO2 pressure to your hoses and fittings, then get a small tub of soapy water. Immerse or apply soapy water around all the fittings and look for bubbling, which would indicate a leak. Resolve all leaks before you start using your system, or your CO2 tank may quickly bleed out.

Filling a Keg

Give your keg a thorough cleaning before use, as many used Cornelius kegs have soda residue present. Pressurize the keg with gas once and check for leaks by applying a small amount of soapy water around the hose fittings and valves. Sterilize the keg with a stainless steel-safe agent such as iodophor before filling. Fill the keg by siphoning from your homebrew fermenter, being careful not to splash or aerate the beer.

Once the keg is full, put the top on it and pressurize the keg using your CO2 tank. Purge any remaining air in the keg and displace it with CO2. Do this by pressurizing the keg with CO2, then release air using the release valve on the top of the keg. Repeat this 4-6 times to make sure that all of the air is out and replaced by CO2. Once the keg has been pressurized with CO2, you can store it in this configuration for several months as long as the keg has no leaks.

Carbonating the Keg

Kegs must be stored under pressure and refrigeration to carbonate properly. I use an old refrigerator to keep three of the 5 gallon kegs on tap at all times, and I've drilled a hole in the side of the fridge so I can keep the CO2 tank on the outside. To calculate the carbonation pressure needed, put a thermometer in your refrigerator and leave it for a few hours. This will give you your carbonation temperature.

Next, using a Carbonation calculator such as BeerSmith (Carbonation tool on the Tools menu), enter the volumes of CO_2 desired to set the carbonation level (2.4 is a good starting number to use), enter the refrigerator temperature and volume of beer. BeerSmith will calculate the CO_2 pressure needed to force carbonate the beer.

If you don't have access to a carbonation tool, start your system at 10 psi of pressure and adjust it to suit your taste later. Set your CO_2 tank regulator to the desired pressure, hook it to your keg and place the keg in the refrigerator. Again, it is not a bad idea to check your lines and connectors for leaks if you have not used the system before. The keg will begin to carbonate in a day or two and reach full carbonation within a week.

Enjoy Kegged Homebrew

You are now ready to enjoy your kegged homebrew! Always pour your beer down the side of the glass and open the tap fully. If you find that the carbonation level is too high, simply dial your CO_2 pressure down a bit. If the beer is too flat, adjust the keg pressure up a bit. Invite some friends over and enjoy fresh homebrew from the tap! Once you move to kegging, it is unlikely you will ever go back to messy bottles.

Malting Barley Grain at Home

For the adventurous home brewer who wants to take all grain beer brewing to yet another level, you can malt your own grains at home. While most micro and home brewers start with malted grain, it is possible to purchase unmalted grains and go through the malting process at home. The equipment required is modest, and bulk unmalted grains can be purchased at a fraction of the cost of malted ones.

Unmalted barley is widely used for animal feed, so a good place to purchase unmalted grains in bulk is likely a local feed store. Usually it is sold in large quantities – typically 50lb to 100lb (22-45 kg) bags. Smaller quantities can be purchased from some brew stores, pet stores or equestrian specialty shops.

There is a lot of variation in unmalted barley quality. If possible, you want to choose a barley that is low in protein as high protein will result in cloudy beer. Inspect the grains if possible before buying to look for minimum broken grains, absence of mold or bugs, consistent color and general overall quality.

Steeping the Raw Barley
The first step in home malting is to steep the barley in water to begin the germination process. Start with a large bucket that can handle the grains plus enough water to float all of the grains. Add water until all of the grains are floating, and let the grains sit in the water for 2 hours.

Remove the grains from the water (a strainer is good for this) and let the grains air out and dry for about 8 hours. This step is important as if you leave the grains in the water they will drown and eventually die.

After the grains have dried for about 8 hours, steep them again in a clean batch of water for another two hours, and dry them again for 8 hours. You will likely have to continue this for a third cycle. Within 24 hours of starting, you should see small roots start to grow from the base of the kernel (called chits). Stop your cycles of steeping and drying once you have 95% of the grains germinated.

You should have added approximately 40-45% moisture (water) at this point. Assuming you started the dry grains with ~9-10% moisture content, adding 35% moisture will result in a weight gain as follows: 1 kg of grain has ~100 g of water before steeping. Adding 350g of water (45% water content) results in a total of 1.35kg. So if you started with a given weight of grains, you can stop steeping when the grains weigh 30-35% (1/3rd) more than when you started.

Germinating the Grains

The grains must now be germinated in a cool, slightly moist, but well ventilated area to grow the small leaflet inside the grain called an acrospire. This generally takes 2-5 days. The ideal temperature for germination is 64F, or about 18C.

You want to keep the seeds cool, spread them out well and moisten them periodically with a little spray mist. The germination process generates heat, which can lead to bacteria or mold growth so it's important to aerate the grains and turn them every few hours in a cool location to avoid infection. Many early maltsters actually spread the grains on a concrete "malting floor" to keep them cool and make it easy to turn them periodically.

You continue malting until the small leaf (acrospires) within the grain is approximately 80-100% of the length of the grain. Note that the acrospires is inside the grain, so you need to actually split the grain open with a knife or razor blade and look for the white leaf that is part of the endosperm and attached to the rootlets. Typically the external portion of the rootlet will be about 2x the length of the grain when it is finished, but checking the actual acrospire length is the best method to determine when to stop.

Drying the Malt

Drying the malt can be difficult as it requires a steady temperature of between 90-125F (31-50C). Drying at a higher temperature will destroy the enzymes needed for mashing. If you are fortunate enough to have an oven with temperature control that can go this low, then leaving it in the oven for ~24 hours is an excellent way to go. In some cases, even the oven light is sufficient to reach the 90F temperature needed, though it may take some time to finish.

If you live in a sunny dry climate, sun drying is also an option. Some care is needed to keep birds and other small scavengers away, but you can leave it out in the sun for 2 days which should be sufficient to dry the malt.

A third option is to use an actual food dehydrator. Inexpensive home food dehydrators are available for as little as $30-40 and work quite well.

You are targeting a finished moisture content of approximately 10%. Assuming you have not lost much material in the first two steps, this would mean the finished weight of the grains with their rootlets attached should be close to the total weight of the unmalted grains before you started the steeping process. Recall that we started with about 10% moisture content in the original unmalted grains. Therefore you can stop drying when the grains plus rootlets weight total approximately their original unmalted weight.

Finishing the Malt

The last step is to separate the dried, malted grains from the rootlets growing out of them. After the grains are sufficiently dry, the rootlets will simply fall off them with a little agitation. You can use a colander or some screen to shake the grains around and separate the dried rootlets. This is a bit of a messy process, as the rootlets tend to get on everything, so you might want to do this outside.

At this point you have pale, malted barley equivalent to that which you would normally purchase from your brew supply store. You can crush it and use it just as you would any pale barley base malt.

If you wish to make specialty malts from your pale barley, you can toast the malts in the oven to make varying shades of crystal, toasted, brown malts. For the lightest of crystal type malts, try toasting at 275F for one hour. For a medium crystal, try toasting at 350F for 15-30 minutes. If you toast at 350F for an hour you will come close to a commercial brown malt. You can also get different variants by toasting wet vs. dry malts. A wet toasted malt will impart a slightly sweeter toasted flavor.

Brewing High Gravity Beers

Want to brew the biggest beers and barley wines? Looking for high gravity ales? In this section we look at the highest gravity ales - barley wines, imperials, high end scotch ale and other highly alcoholic brews.

Planning your Big Beer

High gravity ales start out with a bit of planning. Home brewing big beers is not the same as brewing regular ones. For starters, high gravity ales need malt, and lots of it.

If you are brewing with malt extract, you may need 50-100% more base malt than you usually use. Adjust your recipe to match the desired gravity.

For all grain brewers the situation is more complex. Scaling up the amount of grain you use while keeping the batch size the same will lower your overall batch efficiency. This is because you are sparging with proportionally less water per pound of grain – and extracting fewer sugars in the process. Where you may have a 72% brewhouse efficiency with a regular beer, your high gravity ale may achieve 60% or less.

As a result you need to lower your brewhouse efficiency when estimating the original gravity of your beer. This means you will need more grain than you would get by just scaling up an average beer.

Beer Balance

A second factor to consider when designing your big beer is balance. Here the bitterness ratio (covered earlier) which is the ratio between the original gravity of the beer and IBUs of bitterness, becomes very important. As you add more malt to make your beer big, you need to add proportionally more hops to balance the beer. Otherwise the big malt will dominate your beer, making it too sweet to drink.

To offset this, you need to calculate the bitterness ratio of your beer and compare it to the average bitterness ratio for your desired style. Big beers need big hops – it's not unusual to have 50, 75 or even 100 IBUs for a big beer or barley wine.

Big Beer Yeast

While you may be tempted to toss any yeast into your big beer, many common ale and lager yeasts do not have the tolerance for the high concentration of alcohol found in big beer This could result in a stuck or incomplete fermentation. If you are brewing big, pick a yeast strain that is specifically designed for high gravity beer. Many big beer brewers even use multiple yeast strains or champagne yeast to complete fermentation.

When adding yeast, be sure to use a big yeast starter. Since you have so much malt in the wort, it is critical to have a robust population of active yeast to ferment your big beer. Scale up the size of your starter to match the higher gravity beer – if you are brewing double the gravity then add a double size starter.

Big Beer Considerations

Some additional concerns come into play when you actually brew your beer. When brewing all grain, you need to calculate how much space you need for your mash. The 5 gallon (19 l) igloo coolers used by most home brewers can only accept around 13lbs (5.9 kg) of grain, even with a relatively low water to grain ratio. If you are brewing with more grain you may need a bigger mash tun.

Since you will be mashing and sparging with less water than a normal batch it is important to maximize your efficiency with the grain and water you have. Draining the mash tun slowly and sparging slowly will help your efficiency.

A variation on big beer brewing, called parti-gyle brewing is worth mentioning here. This technique lets you brew two beers from a single mash. After the main high gravity wort is drawn from the mash tun, additional sparge water is added. Then a second batch of wort, with lower gravity, is drawn off and fermented alongside the main ale. For some very high gravity ales, you can even make a third, very light beer from the third runnings off a single mash tun.

Fermenting a big beer can take much longer than a normal beer. As the alcoholic content goes up, the fermentation tends to slow, so careful monitoring of the gravity is important as well as patience. You may not need as much sugar to carbonate your beer, as there will likely be some residual unfermented sugars in the beer itself.

Finally, it can take much longer to condition a high gravity batch. Some barley wines are aged a year or even two years before reaching peak flavor. However, high gravity beers tend to improve greatly with age much like a fine wine. Your patience will eventually be rewarded when you enjoy your big beer.

Chapter 8: Making Better Beer

*"Drunkenness does not create vice, it
merely brings it into view" – Seneca*

In this chapter, we introduce a number of tips for making better beer, including improving your beer clarity, making full bodied beer, troubleshooting your beer and planning seasonal brews year round.

Making Full Bodied Beer at Home

For many beer styles such as traditional ales, browns, porters and stouts, a full body beer style is very desirable. Full body beers have complex character, better head retention and enhanced mouthfeel. Higher body is achieved by raising the final gravity (FG) of a beer without producing an incomplete fermentation. Body can be enhanced by adding unfermentable (complex) sugars, and also by increasing the amount of protein in the brew. Making full body beer at home can easily be done if you use the following four tips:

Use more Carmelized and Roasted Malts

Malts that have been carmelized like caramel or crystal malts have long chains of sugars that are called dextrins. Even lighter caramel malts such as Carapils have dextrins in them. Dextrin sugars are carbohydrates that are almost tasteless, do not ferment, and subsequently remain in the finished beer enhancing the mouthfeel and perceived body to the brew. A pound (0.45 kg) of Carapils or caramel malt will significantly enhance the body of an average 5 gallon (19 l) batch of beer. Malto-dextrin powder is another adjunct that can be added to enhance the amount of dextrin and therefore body of the beer. Roasted malt, chocolate, and special malts have a high proportion of other unfermentable sugars, and similarly increase the finished body while adding sweetness, raising FG, and enhancing flavor. This method works well for malt extract brewers as well as all grain brewers.

Add Unmalted Grains

Unmalted grains and many non-barley grains contain a large percentage of proteins. Examples include Wheat, Oatmeal, Flaked Barley, unmalted barley and undermodified malts. Proteins do not ferment and can enhance mouthfeel. Unfortunately proteins also reduce clarity of the finished beer, so large amounts of protein enhancing ingredients are best used in darker beers (Oatmeal Stout) or beers that are characteristically cloudy (many wheat beers). Note that many unmalted grains such as wheat, flaked grains and unmodified grains require mashing, and are not suitable for steeping in an extract beer.

Use a Higher Mash Temperature

A third method for enhancing beer body is to increase the temperature when mashing. A higher temperature during the saccrification step (convert at around 156-157F or 69C) will reduce the effect of the beta amylase enzyme leaving larger sugar chains in the beer. These long unfermentable sugar chains will remain in the beer resulting in a higher final gravity and enhanced body. If you are using BeerSmith, simply select any of the "Full Body" mash profiles to convert your mash at a higher temperature.

Use a Low Attenuation Yeast Strain

Select a brewing yeast strain with low average attenuation. Low attenuating yeasts will consume fewer complex sugars leaving a higher final gravity and ultimately a beer with more body. Select a yeast with average attenuation below 70% if possible. Examples of low attenuation yeast include many the English and British ale yeasts, Continental ale yeasts and Alt yeast variants.

Combine all four of these methods for your next complex English Ale, Porter or Stout to make a full bodied beer!

Tips for Crystal Clear Beer

A bright, sparkling clear beer is highly prized by beer drinkers, yet clear beer can be elusive for the average home brewer. Commercial brewers use fining agents, filtering, and pasteurization techniques to keep their beer crystal clear – techniques we will cover in the upcoming sections. Using a few simple tips, it is not difficult at all for home brewers to match the clarity of commercial beer.

Before we jump into the tips, let's take a quick look at the main causes of cloudiness in beer. Cloudiness generally comes from one of three sources: tannins, proteins and yeast. Tannins are naturally occurring elements of the barley grain husk that is extracted along with sugars during the mashing process.

Proteins come both from dark grains and also from certain non-barley grains including wheat, oats and flaked barley. Proteins enhance the head retention and body of the beer, but also hurt the clarity of the beer. It is a delicate balance to achieve a full bodied beer without excessive protein

Finally yeast itself is present in the beer during fermentation and will remain suspended in the beer for some time. Most yeast will eventually precipitate to the bottom of the beer, but it takes considerable time for some yeast strains. Tannins, proteins and yeast also contribute "young" off flavors to the beer, so the quicker you can clear your beer the sooner you can enjoy it!

Select Lower Protein Grains

Proteins enhance the body of your beer, but can hurt clarity. Save high protein adjuncts like wheat, flaked barley and very dark malts for wheat and dark beers where clarity is not a significant consideration. If you are brewing a light beer where clarity matters, choose two row pale malt or pale malt extract base and add only enough high protein darker malts to achieve the desired color, body and head retention.

Cool your Wort Quickly

Use an immersion or counter-flow chiller to cool your beer as quickly as possible and result in what is called a "cold break." If you take your wort from boiling to fermentation temperature quickly, the tannins and proteins will form clumps, fall out, and form a thick layer of trub at the bottom of your boiler. The quicker you can cool the wort, the more dramatic the effect. The less tannins and suspended proteins, the clearer your beer will be. Ideally you would like to cool a boiling 5 gallon batch to room temperature in 15 minutes or less.

Choose a Yeast High in Flocculation

Flocculation is defined simply as the rate at which a particular yeast strain will fall out of the beer once fermentation is complete. If you choose a yeast strain with a high flocculation rating, it will clear much more quickly than one with a low flocculation rate. Flocculation should not be your only consideration, but if you have a choice, pick a yeast strain that both matches the style of your beer and has medium to high flocculation.

Cold Store (Lager) your Beer

Storing beer under refrigeration, called laagering, helps to clear beer rapidly. At lower temperatures it is more difficult for the yeast, tannins and proteins to remain suspended. Cold stored beer will clear much more rapidly than beer stored at room temperature. Note that if you are bottling or naturally carbonating a keg, you need to wait for the beer to become fully carbonated before laagering. Otherwise laagering may slow or kill the yeast resulting in a poorly carbonated beer.

Add a Fining Agent

A number of fining agents can be added to the finished beer that will aid in clearing the beer quickly. These agents work by attaching themselves to the yeast, tannins and proteins to help them precipitate to the bottom of your fermenter or bottle more quickly. We'll cover fining agents in detail in the next section.

Using Fining Agents to Improve Beer Clarity

Fining agents added at the end of your boil step or later during fermentation are great tools to rapidly clear your beer. In the previous section, I covered a range of techniques to help clear your beer. For this section, we zero in on one particular technique – the addition of fining agents.

A fining agent is a compound added to beer to aid in precipitating yeast, proteins and tannins. Fining agents generally have large molecules that are positively charged. These charged molecules attach themselves to negatively charged contaminants and then precipitate them out of the finished beer – helping these contaminants rapidly settle to the bottom of the fermenter.

The three haze producing contaminants effected by finings are: suspended yeast, proteins from the malt, and polyphenols that can come from both hops and malt. A fourth cause of haze is microbiological contamination from infection, but finings will do little to help mitigate infection – so cleanliness at every stage is still important.

Finings may be added either at the end of the boil or in the fermenter. Boiled finings, often called "copper finings" should be added in the last 10-15 minutes of the boil, as boiling them longer often reduces their effectiveness. Irish moss and whirlfloc tablets are used at the end of the boil, primarily to precipitate proteins during the cold break.

Finings for the fermenter are added a few days before bottling or racking to precipitate yeast, proteins and polyphenols. These include chillguard, gelatin, isinglass and polyclar. Care must be taken when adding these finings as the large molecules can create an effect called "nucleation" which releases carbon dioxide stored in the beer, and can lead to a gush of rapid foaming. Nucleation is the same process that creates a gusher when you drop mentos into diet soda.

Irish Moss

Irish moss is a dried additive derived from seaweed. It is added in the last 10-15 minutes of the boil to aid in coagulation and precipitation of proteins during the cold break. Approximately 1 tsp is needed per 5 gallons of wort. Irish moss does a great job reducing protein haze in the finished beer, and you can actually see clumps of protein form and drop out at the end of the boil when it is used.

Whirlfloc Tablets

Whirlfloc tablets, like Irish moss, is derived from seaweed, but also includes additional purified carrageenan, which is the active ingredient in Irish Moss. One tablet is added per 5 gallons of wort during the last 10 minutes of the boil. Since it shares the same active ingredients as Irish moss, whirlfloc does a great job precipitating proteins at the end of the boil.

Chillguard

Chillguard is a silica gel that is used in the fermenter a few days before racking or bottling. To use chillguard, dissolve ½ tsp into ½ cup of hot, but not boiling water and gently mix it into 5 gallons of beer. Chilguard is primarily effective for precipitating proteins.

Gelatin

Common unflavored clear gelatin can be purchased from the local grocery store and is effective in reducing both proteins and polyphenols. Gelatin is a collagen based agent derived from hooved animals. Add 1 tsp of unflavored gelatin to a cup of hot, but not boiling water and gently mix it into your fermenter. Again, wait a few days before bottling or racking to allow the gelatin to clear the beer.

Isinglass

Isinglass is also a collagen based additive derived from fish bladders. Used primarily by commercial brewers, isinglass is effective against all three major barriers to clarity: yeast, proteins and polyphenols. Isinglass in its pure form must be mixed with an organic acid before use, but many types of isinglass sold for homebrewer use are so called "instant" variants that come premixed with the acid needed for preparation. Be sure to follow the directions that came with your isinglass. Typical application rates are ½ tsp mixed with 1 cup of hot water per 5 gallons of beer, and allow 4-5 days before racking or bottling.

Polyclar

Polyclar is an additive that consists of powdered PVPP plastic. The plastic is positively charged and very effective at removing polyphenols from finished beer. Polyclar is added in the fermenter at the rate of 2 tablespoons per 5 gallons. Again, the polyclar is usually mixed in a cup of warm water first and then gently mixed into the fermenter. Allow 4-5 days for the polyclar to work before bottling or racking.

The fining agents above are the ones most commonly used by homebrewers. Note that often it is best to use a combination of techniques if you want to attack cloudiness caused by proteins, yeasts, and polyphenols all at once.

I personally use Irish Moss on any beer style where clarity is important, and then use some judgment as to whether to add additional finings at bottling based on the state of the beer at that point.

Filtering Home Brewed Beer

Almost all commercial brewers filter their beer to rapidly improve flavor and clarity. Yet few home brewers filter their beer, either because they lack the equipment or prefer the raw flavor of unfiltered beer. However filtering is a good option for intermediate to advanced brewers who want crystal clear, smooth flavored beer.

Why Filter?

Filtering removes yeast, tannins and some large proteins from the beer that contribute both to off flavors and haze. While many of these impurities will eventually precipitate out of the beer through lagering and aging, filtering accelerates the process by removing them in minutes instead of weeks or months. This is a big reason why commercial brewers use filters – time is money and it is much cheaper for them to filter the beer than store it for weeks or months.

Filtering also has the advantage that it can remove very small impurities from the beer – even those that would not fall out of suspension in the natural aging process. Filters can remove particles as small as 1 micron or even smaller. This can result in a cleaner flavor and much better clarity than is possible with natural aging.

A question many new brewers ask is if they can filter their beer to eliminate the sediment in the bottom of the bottles? The answer is unfortunately no, unless you have some kind of kegging/carbonation system. Filtering the beer removes the yeast from it, so if you filter and then bottle with priming sugar you will just get flat beer. You must have a kegging system to filter your beer.

The only way to filter and bottle beer is to filter your beer into a keg, then artificially carbonate it, and then bottle it from the keg using a counter-pressure bottle filler or beer gun. Also having a pressurized keg makes it much easier to use an inline filter, as gravity works very slowly with typical beer filters.

Choosing a Filter

First, you need to choose a filter size. The filter should be fine enough to filter out tannins and yeast cells, but not too fine or it could alter the flavor of your finished beer. Around 1 micron is the sweet spot for filter size – smaller than 0.5 microns and you risk filtering out some flavor, while larger ones (5 micron and up) may leave yeast in the beer. To filter out bacteria which some commercial brewers do for shelf stability, you need to go to 0.3 microns or below. I don't recommend going below 0.5 microns for home brewing.

Another factor when choosing filter size is how fast your filter may clog. Many commercial brewers actually use a two stage filter. They start with a 5 micron filter to eliminate the large particles and then use a smaller 0.5 micron filter inline as a second stage to filter small particles. If you have a large budget you can do the same, but for a single filter 1 micron is fine.

The most popular beer filters are inline canister filters with a replaceable filter element. These are inexpensive and work well if you have high quality filter cartridges. Some wine filters come in a plate format which offers a larger surface area that is less prone to clogging. I do not recommend using household water filters as these are slow and prone to clogging. Purchase a filter designed for use with beer and change your filter often as the small inline filters clog quickly.

Filtering Your Homebrew

Despite the fact that filtering can be used to accelerate the aging of your beer, you don't want to filter your home brewed beer too early. Some important chemical changes take place during the later phases of fermentation and early aging. If you halt these too early by filtering you will end up with poor flavor balance. Commercial brewers use a additives and techniques that allow them to filter earlier.

Allow the beer to fully complete fermentation and then sit in the secondary for at least 2-3 weeks before filtering, then move it to your keg. The filtering process is very simple if you use two kegs. Place your inline filter in between the full and empty kegs and use low CO_2 pressure to transfer the beer from one keg to the other through the filter.

Once the filtering/transfer is complete, close the top on the second keg, purge the air from the top several times and you can refrigerate and force carbonate it as you normally would with any keg.

Filtering home brewed beers is not always required or even desired, but when you want that extra bit of clarity and clean finish it is a nice alternative.

Enhancing Beer Head Retention

An important characteristic in homebrewed beers is the ability of the beer to retain a nice foamy head for a long period of time. Commercial brewers go to great lengths to improve head retention by a variety of additives. However homebrewers also have access to ingredients and additives that can help your foam last until the last drop.

Note that enhancing head retention is closely related to enhancing the body of the beer. Foam is the result of CO_2 bubbles rising through the beer. These bubbles attach themselves to substances in the beer and form a skin around the bubble. Obviously the more CO_2, the more bubbles, but the goal of the brewer is not bubbles but stability of the head. As foam collapeses, evaporating bubbles tend to solidify the beer near the surface, allowing more beer to be poured with less foaming after a few minutes have passed.

Head stability depends on the presence of substances with low surface tension in the beer which can form stable elastic bubbles. The two primary contributors to head retention are certain high molecular weight proteins and isohumulones (alpha acids from hops). Therefore beers with more proteins that are highly hopped will have higher head retention.

Methods for Improving Head Retention
We will explore the following possibilities:

- The use of body and head enhancing malts such as crystal, wheat, or carafoam
- The altering of the mash schedule to enhance head retaining proteins
- The use of heading agents – additives that enhance head retention
- Addition of high alpha hops – which will increase bitterness, but also increase isohumulones that enhance head retention
- Limiting the use of household soaps on drinking glasses and homebrew equipment
- The use of a nitrogen and CO_2 mix for carbonation and serving
- The shape of the glass used to serve the beer

Head Enhancing Malts
The inclusion of proteins and dextrines enhance the body and head retention of finished beer. Crystal malts to include the light Carapils and Carafoam, as well as all of the caramel malts contribute to head retention. High protein grains such as torrified or flaked barley, wheat and oats also contribute to head retention.

Unfortunately when used to excess, proteins and dextrines can interact with tannins and reduce clarity and promote cloudiness, so a proper balance must be struck. The overuse of such malts can result in proteins reacting with tannins to create a chill haze.   Carapils, Carafoam malted wheat or light caramel malts are preferred for lighter beers, while unmalted wheat, oats and flaked barley should only be used in darker beers where clarity is not a major concern.

Mashing Schedule
Since head retention depends on the level of high molecular weight proteins, any step in the mash that breaks down proteins is undesirable. For example, a protein rest in the 50-60 C (122-140 F) range would not be desirable. To improve head retention you would generally favor a full bodied, higher temperature mash, with main conversion in the 158 F (70 C) range, and avoid intermediate protein rests.

Heading Agents
Homebrew shops sell a variety of additives, usually under the generic title heading agent. Some are intended to be added at bottling time, while others need to be added at the end of the boil. Follow the instructions included with the agent to determine what is required. Many heading agents are derived from an enzyme called pepsin that come from pork.

Other popular heading agents include iron salts, gums, and alginates. All heading agents will alter the flavor of the beer, most often making the character softer. In general, heading agents are not necessary for homebrews that are made from 100% malted barley and wheat. Heading agents are more commonly used in commercial beers that have high rice and corn content, and lack the necessary proteins of an all-malt beer.

Hops
As mentioned in the introduction, isohumulones, which are a form of alpha acid, also will enhance the head retention of beer. Alpha acid is the primary bittering agent in hops. Therefore highly hopped beers such as IPAs will have better

head retention. Obviously overall malt-bitterness balance is still required, but one can use higher levels of hops, particularly in darker full bodied beers to enhance head retention.

Limit the Use of Household Soaps

Household soaps such as common dish soap and dishwashing soap have a significant detrimental effect on head retention in beer. You should not use household soaps on your drinkware. Detergent washed glasses in particular will quickly reduce the head on even a well constructed beer. Instead use a beer-friendly cleaning agent from your local homebrew supplier.

A Nitrogen Mix

Some beers, most notably Guiness Irish Stout, are carbonated and poured with a mix of nitrogen and carbon dioxide. CO_2 is relatively soluable in beer, and therefore does not promote the formation of gas bubbles as well as non-soluable gasses. Nitrogen dissolves less easily in beer, and provides a better base for forming a stable head. However, nitrogen alters the perceived character of the beer, and use of pure nitrogen would result in an unacceptable mouthfeel and carbonation.

A mix, therefore, is always used. The mix varies depending on the style of beer – a low carbonation stout might be served with a mix of 25% carbon dioxide and 75% nitrogen, while ales and lagers might include more CO_2 – perhaps 60% CO_2 and 40% nitrogen. Low carbon dioxide mixes (25/75) can be applied by mixing the gases in the cylinder, but higher mixes generally require two separate tanks – one of CO_2 and one of nitrogen. A high precision blending device either at the tap (i.e. a stout tap) or inline are needed to blend the two gasses for dispensing.

Shape of Serving Glass

The shape of the glass is also a determining factor in both head formation and head retention. A tall narrow glass enhances the formation and retention of the head, while short wide glasses do not. This is the reason many Bavarian wheat beers and

Pilsners are served in tall narrow glasses. Use the proper glass for the style of beer you are pouring to enhance the overall presentation.

Better Beer with the Burton Blow-off Method

In this section, we take a look at a homebrewing technique called the "blow-off method" or Burton Union System for improving your beer. The blow-off method removes proteins, tannins, grain husks, hops and other undesirable materials that tend to form at the top of the fermenter during the early stages of active fermentation.

These materials are an undesirable byproduct of the brewing process, and float or get pushed to the top of the fermenter by carbon dioxide produced during the active stage of fermentation. These undesirables form a separate layer, called the 'Kraeusen' over the beer.

We wish to separate these from the beer as early as possible because tannins, proteins, and other materials will contribute to cloudiness as well as add off-flavors to the beer. Many people use a secondary fermentation or conical fermenters to separate the beer from heavy materials that fall out right after active fermentation. The blow-off method attempts to remove lighter materials that float to the top of the fermenter as early as possible.

The Burton Method

I first read about the blow-off method in Charlie Papazian's book The Home Brewer's Companion (p 172), and have used it successfully for the last 15+ years. Commercial brewers in Burton-on-Trent pioneered the related Burton Union "blow-off" system over 200 years ago and have used it for popular styles like Bass Ale. Their system recovers some of the flocculent yeast from the top fermenting ale and reuses it for later batches. However, the blow-off method used by homebrewers merely discards the kraeusen.

To use the blow-off method, you need a glass or plastic bottle "carboy" fermenter of the same size as your target volume. A 5 gallon (19 l) glass or plastic carboy is ideal. Next, procure several feet of 1″ inner diameter plastic tubing. The tubing should fit tightly in the top of the carboy.

The method is to fill the carboy to the top when brewing and then use the large size tube to "blow off" the early foam and material that rises during active fermentation. A large container with water captures the liquid and material blown out of the fermenter and also acts as a giant airlock. Partially fill the overflow container with water so the end of the tube can be kept under water forming an airlock seal.

Fermentation

Leave this system in place for active fermentation during the first few days, and switch to a smaller airlock or secondary fermenter once activity has died down. You do need to be careful, however, as a smaller airlock will clog up if active fermentation is still ongoing. On one occasion, I switched the airlock before fermentation had completed and ended up blowing the stopper and airlock right off the top of the carboy. It was a huge mess.

If you have a suitable 5 gallon (19 l) carboy, give the blow-off method a try. You will be surprised how much debris collects in your overflow tank and not in your beer.

Troubleshooting Home Brewed Beer

In this section we examine the topic of troubleshooting homebrewed beer. Despite the best laid plans of mice and men, not every beer you brew is going to be a homerun. Homebrewing beer is a combination of both art and science, and sometimes the art or science goes wrong.

Fortunately all is not lost, for each bad batch is an opportunity to learn how to diagnose and improve your next batch.

Assuming you've already taken the time to carefully design your beer and match the target style, the next thing to examine is the taste of your beer. Beer troubles each have their own unique signature which you can evaluate using the guide below.

Bitterness

Excess bitterness in your beer is usually perceived on the back of the tongue, and often manifests itself as a bitter aftertaste. If bitterness is too low the beer often will have a very malty, sweet or grainy profile. Some beers such as IPAs require high bitterness, while others such as Scotch and many German ales require a malty profile.

Excess bitterness is created by overuse of boiling/bitterness hops, long boil times, the use of black or roasted malts, and the use of alkaline water or water with excess sulfates. Conversely low bitterness can result from a low bitterness to gravity ratio, too little hops, malty grains such as Vienna and Munich malts, short boil time or high fermentation temperatures. Filtration can also reduce the bitterness of your beer in many cases.

Body

Body is often referred to as mouth-feel or the thickness of the beer. Full bodied beers have a well rounded thick feel to them while light bodied beers have a thin profile.

In the previous section, we covered how to enhance the body of your beer. Some techniques include adding caramel, crystal or carafoam malts, lactose, malto-dextrin, adding more malt overall, adding wheat, increasing the mash temperature of your beer and fermenting at a lower temperature. Conversely reducing additives, adding rice or sugar, decreasing mash temperature and fermenting at higher temperatures, can create thin beers.

Diaceytl Flavors

Diaceytl flavor comes through as a buttery or butterscotch flavor. It is most often caused by incomplete fermentation. Potential causes include an old or undersized yeast starter, lack of oxygen in the wort before fermentation, lack of yeast nutrients, bacterial contamination or use of excessive adjuncts such as corn or rice that lack proper nutrients. If you prematurely halt fermentation by suddenly raising or lowering temperature, add finings too soon or choose a yeast with very high flocculation you can get a distinct butterscotch flavor in your beer.

You can counteract diaceytl by starting with an appropriately sized yeast starter, make sure your wort is properly oxygenated before fermentation, avoid contamination and making sure a majority of your grain bill contains fresh barley malt with enough diastatic power. Barley malt naturally has the nutrients needed for proper yeast growth.

Alcoholic Profile

The alcoholic profile of a beer is most often perceived as a warm sensation in the mouth and throat. Different styles obviously require different alcohol profiles as indicated by the starting and ending gravities in the BJCP Style Guide (**bjcp.org**). Ideally a beer should have a balanced profile that compliments the overall flavor.

Fusel alcohols leave a solvent like flavor in the beer and are most often produced by fermentation at excessively high temperatures. Fermenting in the recommended range for your yeast can mitigate any solvent-like fusel flavors.

Overall alcohol balance can be controlled by adjusting your original gravity to match the style of beer as well as taking proper care in fermentation to make sure the wort is properly aerated, pitched and kept within the recommended temperature range during fermentation. If there is a significant mismatch between the alcohol content and body of the beer, you can also look at adjusting the body of the beer (described previously) to better balance your recipe.

Astringency

An astringent flavor comes across as grainy or a raw husky flavor. In some cases it may be dry or similar to the flavor of grape skins.

Astringency is most often caused by oversparging your grains or boiling your grains. It can also be caused by sparging with excessively hot water (over 175F), excess trub in the wort, and overmilling of your grains. You can minimize astringency by proper milling, sparging and a good rolling boil when brewing your beer.

Phenolic Flavors

Phenolic flavors are perceived as a medicinal or band-aid like flavor that can be quite harsh. It also sometimes is perceived as plastic, smokey or clove like. Strong phenolic flavors can make the beer undrinkable in some cases.

Phenolic flavors, like astringency, can be caused by oversparging or boiling your grains. In addition the use of chlorinated tap water or presence of bacterial contamination can also cause phenolic flavors. Excessive use of wheat malts or roasted barley malts can also lead to clove like flavors. Check your equipment and bottle caps for leaks and potential contamination, carefully control your sparging process and use an alternate water source if needed to mitigate phenolics.

Dimethyl Sulfide (DMS)

DMS flavors and aromas come across as cabbage, rotten eggs or a sweet corn like aroma. Excess DMS can spoil your beer.

DMS has many potential causes. These include high moisture malt (especially 6 row), bacterial contamination, oversparging at low temperature (below 160F/71C), and underpitching your yeast. Covering your pot during the boil can also create DMS. Storing malt in a cool dry place, care when sparging and boiling, and a proper yeast starter can help to mitigate the ill effects of DMS.

Sour/Acidic Flavors

Sour and acidic flavors may be perceived as a bitter, cider-like, lemon-juice or sour candy flavors usually at the side of the tongue.

One primary cause of sourness is contamination due to inattention to proper sanitation. The use of excessive sugar, particularly refined sugars used by many beginners can also introduce a sour cider-like flavor. Other causes include the addition of excessive ascorbic acid, introduction of bacteria or contamination, excessively high fermentation temperatures and storage of the beer at very warm temperatures.

I hope this beer troubleshooting guide will help you diagnose common brewing problems and their causes.

Seasonal Beer Brewing

For many years, I've wanted to do a better job of matching my beer brewing with seasons and major holidays. But I always found myself behind. When October rolled around it was too late to brew that Oktoberfest, and my green beer was always a bit too late for St Patty's day. My stouts were always finished for the warm summer months.

To combat this, I've assembled a brewing schedule of sorts to help me have mature beers ready for the right holiday or season. To keep it simple, I've listed popular styles of beer for different seasons by quarter, and a corresponding list of which quarter you need to brew them in. The assumption here is that 3 months lead time is enough for me to assemble the ingredients, brew the beer, and have it mature properly. While

I don't brew all of these styles each year, it gives me a list to choose from.

Winter Beer Styles – Beers to Brew in Fall, Drink in Winter:

- Holiday Ales
- Christmas/Winter Beer
- Stouts, Porters and other Dark Beers
- Barley Wine (needs long aging – start a year or more in advance)
- Winter Wheats
- Smoked Rauchbier
- Scotch Ale
- Old Ale

Spring Beer Styles – Beers to Brew in Winter, Drink in Spring

- Irish Ale and Irish Stout
- Green Beer for St Patty's Day
- Bock/Doppelbock
- India Pale Ale
- Fruit Beer
- Wheat Beer, Weizen and Weisse – particularly Hefeweizen
- Saison
- Blonde Ale
- Belgian Wit/White Beer

Summer Beer Styles – Beers to Brew in Spring, Drink in Summer

- Bavarian Weizen/Weisse
- Pilsner
- Cream Ale
- Steam Beer – California Common

- Kolsch Beer
- Summer Ales
- Saison
- Fruit/Wheat Beers

Fall Beer Styles – Beers to Brew in Summer, Drink in the Fall

- Marzen/Oktoberfest
- Pumpkin Beer
- English Pale Ale
- Brown Ales
- Dunkelweizen
- Harvest Ale

A little forethought and planning can lead to timely enjoyment of your favorite beer styles. If you brew your favorite style a few months in advance, it will reach maturity just in time for the holidays.

Chapter 9: English, Scottish and Irish Beer Styles

"May your glass be ever full. May the roof
over your head always be strong, and may
you be in heaven half an hour before the
devil knows you're dead" – Irish Toast

In this chapter, we will explore the history, formulation and design of many popular beer styles from the United Kingdom including English, Scottish and Irish styles. Many of these styles have a long heritage, going back hundreds of years while others are products of the industrial revolution. The surge in microbreweries since the 1980's in the United States has increased the visibility and popularity of these styles in the eye of many American brewers and beer drinkers.

I will note that you often will find American versions of many of these popular UK beer styles. Examples include American Pale Ale, American Browns, American Porters, American IPA and many others. In most cases, these American variations are made in a similar style to their British counterparts, but typically with American varieties of malt and hops. Often you will also find that clean finish American yeast strains are used instead of the more complex British ale yeasts to appeal to US consumers. The net result is an American variation of many classic British styles that generally is has a cleaner and slightly less complex finish for mass appeal.

If you are interested in seeing recipe examples for all of these styles, visit the BeerSmith blog at **BeerSmith.com/blog,** or my recipe site available from the support page on **BeerSmith.com** - I have hundreds of recipes available in virtually any beer style.

English Pale Ale

English Pale Ale is a classic beer style and a personal favorite of mine. In this section, we take a look at how to brew this classic style at home including the history of the style, formulation of recipes and brewing of English Pale Ale.

The History of English Pale Ale

English Pale Ale shares much in common with classic English Bitters. The defining example of the style is arguably Bass Ale from Bass Brewery in Burton on Trent, England. The Bass brewery was established by William Bass in 1777 as one of the first breweries in Burton on Trent.

Pale ale and bitters both are derived from English "real ales" which were widely produced in England in the 18th and 19th century, and originally served with little to no carbonation from hand pumped cellar kegs.

Pale ale can also trace its origins to the start of the industrial revolution in England. The availability of both coal fuel and high quality steel allowed the production of pale colored malts in the early 1700's. Previously, only brown and dark malts with smoky aroma were available due to the use of wood in malting.

The English Pale Ale Style

English Pale Ale has a medium high to moderate hoppy flavor and aroma. Often a malt or caramel flavor and aroma is present, with a slight alcoholic warmth. The hops should balance the caramel and malt flavor at a minimum, though many examples have a slightly hoppy balance.

The body of a Pale Ale is medium to full, and carbonation is generally low except for some bottled commercial or export ales. The finish is dry with no secondary malt flavors, and no diceytl. Fruity esters, often a byproduct of English ale yeast, are often present.

Original gravity is between 1.048 and 1.062, with 30-50 IBUs of bitterness. Color is golden to deep copper (6-18 SRM). Alcohol by volume is a healthy 4.6-6.2%.

Brewing an English Pale Ale

The base malt for English Pale Ale is English pale malt. The preferred type is English two row barley malt with low nitrogen content, traditionally a bit darker than other pale malts due to the use of higher kilning temperatures. Pale malt composes about 90% of the total grain bill. For extract brewers, start with a pale base extract and add the appropriate color steeped caramel malt to achieve your desired color.

Crystal/caramel malts are used in pale ales, both to add color and body. Crystal generally makes up 5-10% of the total grain bill and is selected in a color to balance the overall target color.

Maltose syrup is used in many commercial pale ales, but is hard to find for use in home brewing. Corn or cane sugar can be used in small quantities (generally less than 10%) to give a similar effect.

Wheat, cara-pils, or flaked barley are occasionally used in pale ales to add body. Only a few percent are added, as any larger amount will result in a cloudy finish to the beer. Chocolate and black malts are used very rarely in some recipes, but I recommend not including them in your pale ale.

BC Goldings and Fuggles hops are the favorite varieties for Pale ales. Target, Northdown and Challenger are occasionally substituted. My personal preference is BC Goldings. Often three hop additions are used – one for boiling/bitterness, an aroma addition at the end of the boil and finally dry hops for added aroma after fermentation.

A single step infusion mash is sufficient for mashing a pale ale, as the highly modified English malt will convert easily. A medium to high body mash profile (153-157 F or 67-69C) will give you an authentic rich bodied beer.

For Burton style English Pale Ales, the water profile is extremely high in Calcium Carbonate and Bicarbonate. Burton water has 295 ppm Ca, 725 ppm Sulfate and 300 ppm Bicarbonate. This exceptionally hard water accentuates the bitterness in the hops giving a sharp finish to the beer. For home brewers, a small amount of Gypsum ($CaSO4$) added to the brewing water is sufficient to give a slightly sharper finish.

English Pale Ale yeast is used for traditional Burton ales like Bass, and the major liquid yeast manufacturers even carry a special strain for Burton ales. Other English ale yeasts are also popular with homebrewers for all types of pale ales. Finally, some homebrewers use American ale yeast for its clean finish and neutral flavor.

Pale ale should be fermented and aged at traditional ale temperatures (generally 62-68F), lightly carbonated and served slightly warm if you are a traditional ale fan. American brewers may prefer higher carbonation and a colder serving temperature.

India Pale Ale (IPA)

India Pale Ale (or IPA) is a popular staple of homebrewers, microbrewers and hopheads that enjoy brewing some of the hoppiest beers on the planet. In this section we look at India Pale Ale beer recipes, how to brew an IPA recipe and its history.

History

India Pale Ale traces its origins to the 17th century in England with the earliest pale ales. In fact, new malting techniques developed at the start of the 17th century using coke-fired as opposed to wood-fired kilns enabled production of the first pale malts, and subsequently paler beers. One of the popular pale styles was a beer called October beer, which was highly hopped and designed to be stored for an extended period. Note that this English October beer bears no relation to modern German Oktoberfest beer.

George Hodgson, owner of Bow Brewery brewed a version of October beer that was popular among the traders of the East India Trading Company in the late 1700's. East India traders subsequently started trading many of Hodgson's beers including his October beer. The highly hopped, high gravity, highly attenuated pale ale actually benefitted from the long trip to India and became popular with consumers there.

Other brewers, including several large Burton breweries like Bass, Alsop and Salt lost their European export market in Russia due to new high tarrifs on beer. They quickly emulated the October beer of Bow Brewery and also started exporting to India. The style, which now was now commonly called "India Pale Ale", became popular in England as well around 1840.

The IPA Beer Style

IPA is a hoppy, fairly strong pale ale traditionally brewed with English malt, hops and yeast. The American version has a slightly more pronounced malt flavor and uses American ingredients. The BJCP style guide for 2008 places original gravity at between 1.050 and 1.075, and highly attenuating yeasts are used to drive a final gravity between 1.010 and 1.018 for 5-7.5% alcohol by volume.

Multiple hop additions dominate the flavor profile in IPAs. English IPA's typically have 40-60 IBUs, though the slightly stronger imperial IPA versions can have hop rates as high as 120 IBUs.

Color is similar to many pale ales – golden to deep copper color – varying between 8-14 SRM for the finished beer. Moderate carbonation is often used, though some English IPAs are lightly carbonated.

Brewing an IPA

Hops dominate the flavor of an IPA, so careful selection of the hop additions is critical to success. Traditional English IPAs use popular English hops such as Fuggles, Goldings, Northdown, Target, though sometimes noble hops are also used in finishing. Higher alpha English hops are also popular for bittering. American IPAs use the rough American equivalents such as Cascade, Centennial, Williamette, though again higher alpha hops are often used in bittering.

Multiple hop additions are always used for IPAs including bittering hops at the beginning of the boil, and several additions of finishing hops in the last 5-15 minutes of the boil, with dry hops to provide a hoppy aroma. In general, higher alpha hops are used for the base boil addition while aromatic lower alpha hops are used in finishing and dry hopping, though some traditional IPAs use lower alpha English hops throughout.

Traditional English 2-row pale malt makes up the bulk of the grain bill (or two row American malt for the American IPA), usually around 85-90% of the total. Crystal and caramel malts are used to add color and body to achieve the desired overall color both in extract and all-grain recipes.

Chocolate and black malts are not often used in commercial examples though they occasionally make their way into home-brewed recipes. Personally, I prefer moderately colored caramel/crystal malt. Occasionally you will see wheat, flaked barley or carapils malt added to enhance body, though these are rarely used and only in small quantities.

As many IPAs were first brewed in the English city of Burton, they share much with their English Pale Ale cousins, including the unusual Burton water profile that accentuates the hoppy profile. The Burton water profile has extremely high concentrations of calcium carbonate and bicarbonate.

Depending on your local water source, a small addition of Gypsum (CaSO4) can sometimes help to simulate the hop-enhancing high carbonate Burton waters.

IPAs are most often made with traditional English ale yeasts, though care must be taken to choose a highly attenuating yeast and avoid some of the lower attenuating, fruity British ale yeasts. Many brewers bypass the problem entirely by choosing a highly attenuating American or California ale yeast for a cleaner finish.

All grain IPAs should be mashed at a lower temperature than pale ales to achieve the high attenuation desired. A mash temperature around 150F/65C for 90 minutes will aid in breaking down more complex sugars for a clean finish that accentuates the hops.

IPAs are fermented and stored at the traditional ale temperatures, usually around the mid 60's F. Long storage periods are sometimes required to achieve the proper hop-malt balance.

Brown Ale

Brown ale is a distinctively English style that has also become popular with microbreweries in the United States. Here we're going to look at the origins of this classic style, how to brew Brown Ale at home.

The History of Brown Ale

Brown Ale is an English style without a clear starting date. Many of the earliest English ales were likely brown ales, as most malts were kilned over hardwood fires leaving a distinctly brown color as well as a smoky flavor. Brown malt, though almost extinct today, formed the major part of English ale's for at least 800 years.

The formal use of the term "Brown Ale" is tied to the introduction of Porter in the early 1700's. Brown ale was likely known simply as "Ale" before that since almost all English ales would have been brown prior to 1700 when coal fires and steel made pale malt production possible. The term "Brown Ale" was also used interchangeably for the next 100 years to describe both Porters and Stouts. Brown was in fact a generic term used to describe the insanely popular Porter of this period.

In the early 1800's, some distinction was being made between Stouts, Porters and Milds. In many cases, Brown ale was produced by making a Stout or Porter with the first runnings and then collecting the second runnings of the mash to produce Brown ales. However, throughout the 18th century "brown" was still used extensively to describe Stouts, Porters and other dark beers brewed primarily around London.

The distinct style of "Brown Ale" we know today is a relatively recent invention, though the close relative "Mild Ale" was very popular in the late 1800's and early 20th century. Brown ale emerged in the 20th century as a stronger and sometimes darker version of English mild.

Brown Ale Styles

There are at least three major distinct styles of brown ale which are Northern/Newcastle, Southern/London and American. I've excluded Brown Porter, which is a variation of Porter. Northern or Newcastle brown ales have an original gravity between 1.040 and 1.052, dark amber color between 12 and 22 SRM and bitterness of 20-30 IBUs. Both malt and bitterness are present in moderate levels, and caramel/malt flavor adds some sweetness. Newcastle Brown Ale is the obvious example, though a number of Nut Brown Ales also fall into this category.

London or Southern Brown ales are malty with relatively low bitterness. They have a sweet caramel flavor, very dark color and some dark fruit (raisin) flavors. They are made with an original gravity between 1.035 and 1.042 and low bitterness level of 12-20 IBUs with dark color of 19-35 SRM.

American Brown ales are brewed with a higher starting gravity between 1.045 and 1.060 with higher bitterness of 20-40 IBUs. Like London Brown, they have a dark color between 19 and 35 SRM. They have medium maltiness and body, are slightly dry, and have higher bitterness and aroma than their British counterparts. Not surprisingly, American hop varieties are often used.

Brewing Brown Ales

Many brewers take an "everything but the kitchen sink" approach to brewing browns, but Ray Daniels argues that superior results can be obtained by focusing on a few key ingredients along with proper yeast and water selection.

Brown ales are made from a base of English pale malt. Crystal malt is almost always used in brown ale, averaging about 10-15% of the total grain bill. Chocolate malt, too, is used but sparingly – making up from 3-6% of the grain bill. Black and roasted malts are seldom used in brown ales, and if used make up as little as 2% of the grain bill.

Homebrewers use a variety of specialty malts to add character including aromatic malt, biscuit malt, wheat malt, toasted malt, special B, oatmeal and others. In some cases these specialty malts can make up as much as 5-15% of the grain bill. Commercial browns typically take a simpler approach using only 1-2 dark malts to provide the bulk of color and character.

A single infusion mash in the 152-154F (~67C) range targeting a medium body beer is appropriate for all brown styles.

English brown ales have low bitterness and are therefore lightly hopped. Popular English hops such as Goldings, Fuggles, and sometimes Tettnanger are often used. American browns are much more highly hopped, in some cases approaching levels twice that of typical English browns. Cascade is most popular; though Perle, Williamette, and other American hop varieties may also be used. For American browns, hops are often added at several different stages including occasionally dry hopping.

Yeast selection also depends on the style of brown you are brewing. American browns are typically made with dry American Ale or German Ale yeast with a high attenuation. English browns use the full range of UK ales including London, Irish Ale, and other full body English Ale yeasts to add character, esters and the unique mix of English complexity.

Water high in carbonates is desirable, especially for the English styles. London was the home of dark ales for the past 250 years largely due to its high carbonate water. Sulfates, however, are undesirable so minimize the use of gypsum. American browns often use lower carbonate water than their English cousins.

Brown ales are fun to brew, and offer a wide variety of interpretations for the creative brewer – so make your next batch a brown ale.

Scotch Ale

Scotch Ale brings forth visions of fog filled bogs, dimly lit pubs and a hearty pint of ale. Scotland has always had its own distinct brewing style with an array of unique beers from the 60/- shilling light Scottish ale to the "wee heavy" strong ales. In this section we examine the history of Scotch ales as well as some Scottish ale beer recipes.

Scotch ale can be divided into roughly four categories. The standard ale is available in three strengths: light, heavy and export. A fourth category is often broken out for strong Scottish ales or "wee heavy" ales. These ales are also often named by their 19th century per-barrel price in schillings (now obsolete) as 60/-, 70/- and 80/- for the light, heavy and export and higher numbers of 100/- to 160/- for strong and "wee heavy" styles.

The History of Scottish Ales

Scotland has traditionally produced a wide array of beer styles including many that are either English or Irish in character. During the 18th and 19th centuries Scotland was a major exporter of all kinds of beer to both England and also its colonies, and Scotland was first in the British Isles to begin producing lager in large quantities.

Despite the influence of neighbors, Scotland's unique geography and political situation combined to produce a uniquely Scottish style of beer that we now know as Scotch ale. According to Daniels, in <u>Designing Great Beer</u>, two of the major factors were the availability of malt and hops. Barley has always been grown in Scotland, with a large portion dedicated to the production of whiskey. However, in Southern Scotland significant portions of the yearly crop were dedicated to beer production.

Hops, however, have never thrived in Scotland. The soil and conditions are poor for hop production, so hops had to be imported often from England at high expense. As a result a variety of hop alternatives were traditionally used including spices, herbs and quassia. Later, when hops were used, they were added only sparingly resulting in a distinctly malty character. This countrasts with the area to the south in England where malt was heavily taxed and hops plentiful resulting in more highly hopped styles such as IPA.

A look at the historical brewing of Scottish ales reveals that these ales were mashed with one or at most two steps, usually at high temperature (often above 160F/71C!) and sparged slowly and often fermented at relatively cold temperatures. The combination no doubt produced a beer full of body and resulted in very low attenuation of the yeast. Bitterness was low, and attenuation also low, resulting in a malty full bodied beer. The finished beer was aged only a few weeks and then shipped directly to pubs for consumption. When aged, the beer was often kept cold which aided in enhancing clarity.

Brewing a Scottish Ale

As mentioned above Scottish ales have four major categories. The three traditional Scotch ales are distinguished primarily by strength and bitterness: original gravity for 60/- light is in the range 1.030-1.035, for 70/- heavy it is 1.035-1.040 and 80/- export comes in at 1.040-1.054. Strong Scotch "wee heavy" ales have very high gravities in the 1.070-1.130 range.

Bitterness is low – with about 10-15 IBUs for light and ramping up to 15-30 IBUs for the export version. Even the strong ales have a low bitterness in the 17-30 IBU range. Malty and caramel flavors dominate the style with little to no hop aroma or flavor.

Scotch ales have an amber to light brown color. All have a target color in the 9-17 SRM range, though the strong ale may be darker (up to 25 SRM) due to the large amount of malt added.

Formulations for Scotch ales vary, but they all start with a pale malt or pale extract base, generally making up about 70-80% of the grain bill. Crystal malt is used in both commercial and homebrewed recipes making up from 5-10% of the grain bill. Black or roast malt provide color and character in the 2% range, though most purists prefer roast malt to black malt.

Interestingly almost all commercial examples use either wheat malt or sugar in the 5-10% range, though sugar is rarely added to homebrewed versions. Other commonly added homebrew grains in small amounts include chocolate malt, carapils for body, munich and amber malts though these are not commonly added to commercial versions.

There are no specific hops tied to the Scotch style, though low alpha traditional English or Continental hops are considered most appropriate. Goldings, Williamette and Fuggles are often used commercially, though noble hops such as Hallertauer or Saaz can also be used. Bitterness and hop flavor should be kept to a minimum, so use just enough hops to balance the malt.

The selection of Scotch yeast is not as important as the fermentation method. Scotch ales are fermented at much lower temperatures (50-60F or 10-16C) than traditional ales, and the fermentation can take several weeks to complete as a result. After fermentation, the ale is cold aged to aid in clarity. This produces a very malty but clean beer profile. You also want to select a low attenuation yeast that can handle the lower temperatures.

Though Edinburgh is famous for its pale ales and hard water, high sulfate water is not a critical element in brewing Scotch ale and in fact can be detrimental as it brings out the hop sharpness too much. I recommend a moderate neutral water profile low in sulfates that will support the malty base and not enhance the hops excessively.

The Porter Style

Porter is an English beer style that has become very popular in the United States. Here we will look at the origins of Porter, how to brew Porter at home and provide a collection of sample recipes. When I started brewing back in the 1980's, the microbrewery revolution was still in its infancy, and it was difficult to find anything beyond the classic American lager in the stores. Yet, dark beers were a passion of mine, and Porter was a perennial favorite.

History

Porter is first mentioned in writings in the early 1700's, and the name Porter is derived from its popularity with London's river and street porters. There are many stories surrounding the origins of Porter, such as one about it being a blend of three other beers, but more likely Porter was derived from strong brown ales of the period. Original porters were substantially stronger than modern versions. Wikipedia mentions that hydrometer measurements on 18th century Porters indicate original gravities near 1.071, or 6.6% ABV – about twice the alcohol of a modern beer.

Taxes during the Napoleonic wars drove the alcohol content down to modern levels. Porter was also the first large scale beer to be entirely aged before delivery, often remaining in vats or casks for 18 months before shipment to pubs. As the 1800's started, breweries mixed aged porter with new porter to reduce storage costs. Stouts started as a stronger, darker version of Porter, with most including the name "Stout Porter". Eventually the "Porter" tag was dropped giving the modern style of "Stouts".

In another interesting side note, Porter's popularity was so high that it was stored in huge vats in the late 1700's, and there was an arms race of sorts between major breweries to see who could build the largest vats. According to Ray Daniels book Designing Great Beers, the largest vats approached 20,000 barrels (860,000 gallons) at the end of the 1700s. This compares to the largest in the world today, which clocks in at around 1600 barrels, less than 1/10th the size. In October of 1814, a huge vat at the Meux brewery ruptured and reportedly wiped out an adjacent tank that devastated the neighborhood in a 5 block radius. In the ensuing chaos, at least 8 people were killed.

Designing a Porter Recipe

Designing Porter recipes can be a lot of fun as the Porter style includes room for experimentation. Porters have an OG of 1.040 and up, color of 20-40 SRM and bitterness of 18-35 IBUs for Brown Porter, or up to 55 IBUs for higher gravity Robust Porter. The color is brown to black, and they have low to medium hop flavor. They are almost always brewed with a full bodied mash schedule (higher mash temperature of 154-158F or 68-70C) to give a full body taste. They have low ester, fruitiness and diacytl, are well balanced and have low to medium carbonation.

Traditional porters start with a Pale malt base, and typically add a mix of Crystal, Brown, Chocolate and Black malts to achieve a dark color and taste. Roasted malts are used only in Robust Porter styles. Pale malt makes up 40-70% of the grain bill (60-80% for malt extract brewers). Dark Crystal/Caramel malts are used for color and body and provide at least 10% of the grain bill. Chocolate and Roasted malts each average around 5% of the grain bill, with roasted malt less common in Brown Porter.

A variety of grains including Munich malt, Roasted malt, wheat and additives are also used. I will occasionally brew "kitchen sink" Porter which consists of whatever malts I have laying around over a pale malt base. Traditional Porter also made heavy use of Amber and Brown malts, though these are less commonly used today. Ray Daniels recommends a mash temperature of 153F/67C, though I often go a bit higher (156F/69) to provide a full bodied beer.

Traditional English hops are the appropriate choice for Porter with East Kent Goldings being a favorite of mine. Other good choices include Fuggles, Northern Brewer, Northdown and Williamette. Light dry hopping is appropriate to the style, though hop aromas should not be dominant. English ale yeast is traditionally used for Porter for its fruity flavors, though other high attenuation yeasts are appropriate. Irish ale yeast is also occasionally used by homebrewers. Adjuncts are only rarely added to specialty Porters. A London water profile (high in carbonates) is best.

Dry Irish Stout

Irish Stout is a "strong beer." It is the antithesis of "light beer" and polar opposite of popular American pilsners with its opaque black color and strong, dry coffee-like flavor. The classic Irish Stout is Guiness Stout of Guiness Brewery in Ireland, known the world over for its unique flavor and frothy white head.

The History of Stout

Irish Stout traces its heritage back to Porter. As described previously in the section on the Porter Beer style, Porters were first commercially sold in the early 1730s in London and became popular in both Great Britain and Ireland.

The word Stout was first associated with beer in a 1677 manuscript, with a "stout" beer being synonymous with "strong" beer (Ref: Wikipedia). In the 1700's the term "Stout Porter" was widely used to refer to a strong version of Porter. The famous Guinness brewery in Ireland started brewing "Stout Porter" in 1820, though they previously brewed both ales and Porters. Around 1820, Stout also began to emerge as a distinctive style, using more dark brown malt and additional hops over popular porters of the time. At around the same time, black malt was invented and put to good use in Porters and Stout Porters.

Throughout the 1800's Stout continued to refer to "Strong" – therefore, one could have "Stout Ales" as well as "Stout Porters". However, by the end of the 19th century, "stout" became more closely associated only with dark Porter, eventually becoming a name for very dark beers.

Traditional stouts of the 1800's and early 1900's differ considerably from their modern counterparts. The characteristic Roast Barley that gives Irish stout its dry roasted taste was not widely used until the early to mid 1900's. Some Stouts had very high gravities – 1.070 to 1.090 for many recipes from 1858 cited by Ray Daniels. They also had very high hop rates, in some cases approaching 90 IBUs.

As Pale ales and later European lagers became more popular in the 1800's, sales of both Porter and Stout Porter declined, remaining popular in Ireland and a few other localities in the UK.

The definitive modern Irish Stout is Guinness Extra Stout. Other popular commercial stouts include Beamish Irish Stout and Murphy's Irish Stout. Founded in 1759, Guinness brewery at St James gate in Dublin Ireland has operated continuously for over 250 years under family ownership. Guinness is a classic Irish or Dry Stout style, with a distinctive dry, almost coffee like flavor derived from Roasted Barley. Guinness is brewed in two main forms, the domestic draft version having much lower alcohol content (3.9%) than the export bottled version (6%).

A number of other stout styles are popular including (Russian) Imperial Stout, Oatmeal Stout, Milk Stout, and Chocolate Stout. However for this section, we will stick with the classic Irish Stout style.

Designing and Brewing an Irish Stout

Irish Stout has an original gravity in the 1.035-1.050 range, with domestic versions being at the low end and export versions at the high end of that range. Bitterness is moderate, but must balance the strong flavor of the dark grains used. It should be hopped at a moderate rate of 1 IBU per point of OG (so a beer with 1.040 OG should have 40 IBUs). Color is an extremely dark brown that looks black in the glass – from 35-

200 SRM. Traditionally Irish Stout is served at very low carbonation (1.6-2.0 volumes) and often served warm.

The key ingredient in a classic Irish Stout is Roasted Barley (also called Stout Roast). Roast Barley gives Irish Stout its classic dry coffee-like flavor, deep dark color, and white foamy head. Unlike other dark malts, Roast Barley is made from unmalted barley grain that is roasted at high temperature while being lightly sprayed with water to prevent it from burning. Roast Barley is intensely dark, around 500-550 L, but the unmalted barley produces a white head on the beer as opposed to the darker head made by other malts.

In many commercial dry stouts, Roast Barley is the only specialty grain used. For a Dry Irish Stout, Roast Barley makes up around 10% of the grain bill. Those that don't use Roast Barley use Black malt as a substitute.

Irish Stout is famously full bodied, so the second most popular ingredient is a specialty grain to enhance the body of the beer. Guinness uses Flaked Barley at a proportion of around 10% of the grain bill. Flaked Barley adds significant body and mouthfeel to the beer, but it must be mashed. If you are a malt extract brewer, crystal malt or Carapils would be a good substitute for Flaked Barley.

Many award winning all grain stout recipes also use oatmeal (6% of grain bill range) or wheat (6% range) either in place of flaked barley or as an addition to further enhance the body of the finished beer. Other popular specialty grains include black and chocolate malts, though these are used in small proportions primarily to add complexity to the flavor.

English pale malt (or Pale Malt Extract) makes up the bulk (60-70%) of the grain bill. For all-grain brewers, a medium to full bodied mash profile is desirable. A single step infusion mash is sufficient for well modified English malts. Conversion mash temperatures in the 153-156 F (67-69C) range are appropriate.

The most popular Irish Stout hops by far is East Kent Goldings, though other English hops such as Fuggle, Challenger, Northdown and Target. American varieties such as Cascade are sometimes used by American microbreweries. A single hop addition is made at the beginning of the boil for bitterness. Hop aroma is not a significant factor, so aroma hops are rarely added to Irish Stout.

Irish Ale yeast is historically used in Irish Stout. An ideal yeast would yield an attenuation around 76% for dryness, but many Irish ale yeasts yield a lower attenuation. Some brewers select neutral yeasts with a higher attenuation to achieve a drier flavor profile. London and Whitbread yeasts are also popular choices.

Some Irish Stout recipes, including Guinness use a small amount of soured beer to add a little extra bite and flavor. Refer to the earlier section on souring your wort if you want to duplicate this by souring a few quarts and adding them to your fermented beer.

Finally, few stout fans will forget the smooth creamy head that a draft pint of Guinness has on it. The secret is that Guinness on tap is not served under CO_2 alone, but has a mix of CO_2 and nitrogen. The nitrogen gives it the extra creamy long lasting head. You can serve kegged beer with nitrogen and CO_2 at home, but it requires a separate tank of nitrogen in addition to a tank of CO_2 and also a special "stout tap" to mix the gas when serving.

Russian Imperial Stout

Many people are surprised to find that Russian Imperial Stout is actually an English beer style, but the style was invented and brewed in England for many years. In fact, even today, Russian Imperial Stout is rarely found in Russia.

History

Imperial Russian Stouts were brewed in England for the export to the court of the Tsars of Russia in the 18th century. A high, malty alcohol content and high hop rate were intended to preserve the beer and also prevent it from freezing during its shipboard trip across the Baltic Sea. Thrale's brewery of London brewed the style preferred by Catherine II's court in Russia.

Later Thrale's brewery changed hands and was taken over by Courage, renaming the beer as Courage Imperial Russian Stout. The style has a high alcohol content of 9-10% alcohol by volume. High gravity Russian stout's are also brewed by Guiness and Boston Beer Company (Samuel Adams).

The style was regularly brewed in the 18th and early 19th century before falling out of favor, but this beer has enjoyed a resurgence in the last few years with the rise of microbreweries.

The Russian Imperial Stout Style

Russian Imperial Stout is a robust, deep, complex beer with full bodied flavor. It has a rich dark malt flavor that may vary from dry chocolate to slightly burnt. A slight alcoholic warmth is normal. It may have a fruity profile including complex dark fruits such as plum, raisin or prune flavors. Like many British beers, it can have a caramel, bready or toasted flavor as well with roast malt complexity.

Color ranges from dark brown to jet black (30-40 SRM). Alcohol content is usually high (8-12% alcohol by volume) with a high starting gravity (1.075 to 1.115 OG). Bitterness generally runs high to balance the malty flavor (50-90 IBUs), but hop flavor should only be low to medium overall. Many US versions have higher bitterness. Carbonation is generally low to moderate.

Brewing an Imperial Stout

Imperial stouts start with a well-modified pale malt base, generally using UK pale malts. The pale base typically makes up 75% of the grain bill. Roasted malts of all kind are added, usually comprising of a mix of moderately colored caramel malt, chocolate malt and roast malt to provide complexity, body and flavor. Together these make up the remaining 25% of the malt bill. Other malts such as Munich and aromatic are used in rare cases.

Traditional variations use classic English hops such as Fuggles or BC Goldings, though American microbreweries often also use US hop variants. Hops are typically added as a single boil addition, since a lingering hop aroma and flavor is not needed here. Instead, a high hop rate during the boil provides the bitterness needed to offset the malt.

Since roast malts provide a very acidic addition, it is not uncommon to use slightly alkaline water when brewing imperial stouts. Traditionally, English Ale yeast or Imperial Stout yeast provides the fruity complexity required for this style, though again some American variants use high attenuation US yeast variants for a cleaner finish. Very high gravity options may require high gravity yeast such as champagne or barley wine yeast.

Imperial stouts are fermented at ale temperatures in the 63-68F (17-20C) range, carbonated at low to moderate carbonation rates, and stored at ale temperatures or lower (as they were during the icy trip across the Baltic). Often Imperials require an extended aging period to achieve full maturity due to the high starting gravity.

Chapter 10: Continental Beer Styles

"Beer – Now there is a temporary
solution." – Homer Simpson

In this chapter, we will move from the United Kingdom to the European continent. The European styles often have a completely different character than English ales, with lagers and wheat beers dominating. In addition, continental ingredients including Vienna, Munich, Wheat and Pilsner malts are used often in combination with noble hop varieties. Lager or wheat yeasts are fermented at lower temperatures, and beer is typically lagered (cold stored) for an extended period before serving. Continental styles are also often more highly hopped than their English counterparts.

Bohemian Pilsner

Pilsner beer is remarkable not only for its modern dominance, but also its relatively recent origins. The popularity of Pilsner is truly worldwide phenomena, so much so that Pilsner recipes still dominates the US and many other beer markets. It is simply the most popular beer style in the world.

Pilsner's origins can be traced to a single date and location. On November 11th, 1842, in the town of Pilsen the first keg of Pilsner Urquell was tapped. This makes Pilsner one of the younger beer styles, even among lager beer styles, which were brewed in nearby Bavaria back to the 1500's.

The city of Pilsen in Bohemia (modern day Czech Republic) had a unique combination of ingredients and circumstance to create the Pilsner style. First, the surrounding country produced light 2-row Monrovian barley, considered the finest light malt for brewing beer. Second, the country produced hops originally known as Zatac red, now called Saaz. Saaz hops are a noble hop prized for aroma.

Third, Pilsner had extremely soft water that is desirable for making very pale beers, and the water also enhances the bitterness from the hops. Finally, Bohemian Pilsner shared many brewing techniques with nearby Bavaria. The first Pilsner was created with a combination of these four elements and the important fifth element of Bavarian lager yeast. The result was the palest of lagers with a refreshing aromatic hop finish that we now know as Pilsner.

The Pilsner Style

The defining example of Pilsner is the original Pilsner Urquell from the Pilsner Urquell brewery in Pilsen, Czech Republic. In fact the word Pilsner is reserved in Bohemia exclusively for brewers in Pilsen.

Pilsners have an original gravity between 1.044 and 1.056, very light color of 4-6 SRM and hop rate of 35-45 IBUs. They have light to medium body, a clean flavor and finish with low diaceytls. They are hoppy and slightly malty with no aftertaste. They are typically well carbonated, and often served in a tall Pilsner glass to enhance the perception of carbonation.

Brewing Pilsner Beer

The unusually pale color of Pilsner derives from the use of Monrovian Pilsner malt that is malted at the brewery at the low temperature of 100-122F (38-50C) versus 170-180F (77-82C) for an average lager malt. The lower temperature develops less melodin and a far lighter color than conventional lager malt. It also leaves some residual moisture that will spoil Pilsner malt if not used quickly.

Monrovian Pilsner malt is most desirable for brewing Pilsners, though it can be difficult to find here in the US. Pilsner malt from other sources is an acceptable alternative, and lager malt can be used in a pinch, though it will result in a darker beer than true Pilsner malt.

Brewing light colored Pilsner from extract can be a challenge as extracts are inherently darker than corresponding grain malts due to the extraction process. The best course of action is to choose the lightest possible pilsner or lager malt extract you can find if you want an authentic light pilsner color.

Pilsner Urquell uses 100% pilsner malt, with no other additions. Some home brewers will use a small amount (<10%) CaraPils or very light Crystal malt to add body and head retention.

Pilsners use a Bavarian style three step decoction, though Pilsners typically are mashed with unusually thin decoctions, and then boiled for an extremely long time (often 2-3 hours) to boil off the excess water added. However, many modern commercial and home brewers use a single step infusion mash at 153 F (67 C) with equally good results. Some do add a protein rest.

Saaz hops is used exclusively on traditional Bohemian Pilsners, with hops added at the start of boil and the last hop addition about 30 minutes before the end of the boil.

Soft water is a key ingredient in Pilsner. Pilsner water has extremely soft water containing only 50 parts per million of hardness. For homebrewers, you can often start with distilled water and add the minimal water additions needed to approximate Pilsner water.

Bohemian Lager yeast is the ideal yeast to use for a full bodied Bohemian style, though in a pinch Bavarian or another continental lager yeast can be used for a lighter, drier taste. Your lager should be fermented at 50F and lagered at low temperature of 35-40F for three to five weeks before serving.

Belgian Wit Beer

Belgian Wit is a wonderful light, refreshing beer that narrowly avoided extinction to become a popular hit here in the United States. In this section, we'll take a look at the history, brewing and recipes for Belgian Wit and White Beer.

History

Belgian Wit goes by many names, all variations of the term "White Beer". In French it is called "Biere Blanche", while the Flemish name is Wit or Witbier which is pronounced "Wit" or "Wet". While the style was likely derived from the Belgian Monastery tradition, it reached widespread popularity in the 18th and 19th century in the towns east of Brussels. The two beers "Biere Blanche de Louvain" and "Blanche de Hougerde" were brewed in Louvain and Hoegaarden respectively. The Louvain version was more popular.

After the lager revolution in the 1800's and into the 1900's, Wit gradually declined in popularity and in fact disappeared when the last Belgian Wit brewery went out of business in 1957. Nearly 10 years later, Pierre Celis raised money from family members to open a brewery called De Kluis and began brewing a traditional Wit called appropriately "Hoegaarden".

In 1985, the De Klius brewery burned to the ground, again threatening Witbier with extinction. Pierre Celis was able to raise money from commercial sources to rebuild the brewery, but by 1987 these larger brewers essentially took control from Pierre Celis and altered the recipe to appeal to a broader audience. Pierre Celis, disappointed, moved to Austin Texas where he opened a new brewery making "Celis White" based on the original Hoegaarden recipe.

Brewing The Wit Beer Style

Belgian Wit is a light, wheat based beer with light to medium body, slight sweetness and a zesty orange-fruity finish. It has a clean crisp profile, low hop bitterness and high carbonation with a large white head. Traditional Wit is slightly cloudy due to the use of unmalted wheat, and pale to light gold in color.

Original gravity is in the 1.044-1.052 range, bitterness in the 10-20 IBU range and color in the 2-5 SRM range. Carbonation is high.

Belgian Wit is made from a base of around 50% pale malt, and 50% unmalted wheat. Often, 5-10% rolled or flaked oats are added to enhance body and flavor.

Unmalted wheat presents some challenges for the single infusion homebrewer. Pure unmalted wheat will not convert well with a single infusion mash. This can be rectified by using a multi-step infusion or multi-step decoction mash, but simpler solutions exist. If you substitute flaked or torrified wheat, you can perform a single infusion mash easily, while still preserving the distinctive flavor of unmalted wheat.

If you are brewing from extract, wheat extract might be an acceptable option, but all grain brewers should avoid using malted wheat, as it will not result in the authentic wit flavor. If you desire oats, rolled oats are best if you are brewing all-grain as these two will work well in a single infusion mash. Where possible, high diastatic power pale colored malt should be used as the pale base.

Hops are typically chosen to minimize the hop profile. Low alpha hops such as BC Goldings, Hallertauer, Fuggles or Saaz with just enough hops to balance the sweetness of the malt. I recommend 1 oz (28 g) of BC Goldings boiled for 60 minutes in a 5 gallon (19 l) batch. Dry hopping and late hop additions are not really appropriate for this style.

Spices play an important role in Wit. Coriander and Bitter (Curaco) orange peel are used in small amounts at the end of the boil to add a bit of spice. In some cases, small amounts of sweet (traditional) orange peel are also added, though sweet orange peel should not be a dominant flavor.

The coriander should be cracked, but not crushed, whole seeds. I run my coriander seeds through the grain mill to crack them in half. Bitter Curaco orange peel is not the type you find in the supermarket, but is available from most major brewing supply shops. I recommend about 3/4 ounce (21 g) of bitter orange peel and 3/4 ounce (21 g) of coriander for a 5 gallon (19 l) batch added 5 minutes before the end of the boil.

Since this is one of my favorite styles, I've included my personal recipe for 5 gallons (19 l) of Wit, though you can find many more recipes on our **BeerSmith.com** recipe site:

- 4.5 lb (2 kg) Belgian 2 row Pale Malt
- 4.5 lb (2 kg) Flaked Wheat
- 1 oz (28 g) East Kent Goldings Hops (5%), boiled for 60 minutes
- ¾ oz (21 g) Corriander seed – cracked open and boiled for 5 minutes
- ¾ oz (21 g) Bitter Orange Peel (Curaco orange) – boiled for 5 minutes
- 1 package of Belgian Wit Yeast (White Labs #WLP400) with a starter

Belgian Trappist Dubel and Tripel Ales

Trappist ale is a beer brewed originally by Trappist monks. The style and its substyles (Enkel, Dubbel and Tripel) have also been popularized by many microbreweries over the last 30 years. In this section, we take a look at the popular Trappist style and how to formulate recipes to brew this beer at home.

The History of Trappist Beer

Trappist ale has its clear origins with Trappist monasteries. From the early middle ages, monastery brew houses produced beer throughout Europe both to feed the community and later for sale to fund other church works. The Trappist order, which took its name from La Trappe Abbey in France, was founded as part of the Cistercian order in 1663, though it did not formally separate from the Cistercian order until 1892. The La Trappe Abbey had its own brewery as early as 1685.

Today there are only seven Trappist monasteries that brew beer and six of them are located in Belgium while one is in the Netherlands. The six in Belgium are the most well known, which is why Trappist ales are categorized as Belgian ales. In the late 20'th century, many breweries worldwide started labeling their beer as "Trappist" in response to the popularity of the ales, forcing Trappist abbeys to form the International Trappist Association who's goal is to prevent non-Trappist commercial companies from using the name. They created a logo and convention for true Trappist beers, which must be brewed within the walls of a Trappist abbey by monastic brewers, and the profits from brewing must go to charitable causes and not financial profit.

Due to the popularity of Trappist ales, many commercial brewers still brew similar style beers which are typically sold under as Belgian Dubbels and Tripels.

The Trappist Style

Trappist beers may be divided into four sub-styles. By tradition, most of the true Trappist ales are bottle conditioned. These include:

- **Patersbier** – "Father's beer" which is brewed for the monks and intended for consumption by the monks within the abbey walls. Occasionally this may be offered on site to guests. It is a relatively weak beer in the tradition of Trappist austerity.
- **Enkel** - "Single" beer which was traditionally used to describe the brewery's lightest beer. This is a very close

relation to the Patersbier. Currently, the term is rarely used, and I am not aware of any abbeys that currently produce this style for commercial sale.

- **Dubbel** – "Double" beer. Dubbels are a strong brown ale with low bitterness, a heavy body, and a malty, nutty finish with no diacytl. These beers have a starting gravity of 1.062-1.075 and 6.5-8% alcohol by volume. Color runs the range from dark amber to copper color (10-17 SRM) and bitterness from 15-25 IBUs. This style is also widely brewed by commercial brewers.
- **Tripel** – "Triple" beer. Tripel's are the strongest Trappist ales, running from 7.5-9% alcohol by volume with a starting gravity of 1.075-1.085. They are highly alcoholic, but brewed with high carbonation and high attenuation yeasts to reduce the taste of alcohol. Color runs lighter than Dubbels in the range of 4.5-7.0 SRM and bitterness from 20-40 IBUs, though most Tripels have 30+ IBUs.

Brewing Trappist Style Ales

I'm going to focus on the Dubbel and Tripel styles as these are the only ones brewed commercially today. For both Dubbel and Tripel, Belgian pilsner malt makes up the base ingredient. For Dubbels, sometimes Belgian pale malt may also be used as a base.

For Dubbels, the grain bill can be complex with Munich malts added for maltiness (up to 20%), Special B malt to provide raisin flavor, and CaraMunich for a dried fruit flavor. Also, dark candi sugar is used both to boost alcohol and add rum-raisin flavors. The sugar also allows for a cleaner finish and less alcohol flavor than would be possible with an all-malt beer. Despite the complex spicy flavor of the finished beer, spices are not used.

Tripels being lighter in color typically use a less complicated malt bill. Starting with a pilsner malt base, they add up to 20%

white candi sugar but typically lack the complex array of malts used for Dubbels.

One of the main ingredients that makes Trappist ales unique is the yeast. Both Dubbels and Tripels use special Belgian yeast strains that produce fruity esters, spicy phenolics and higher alcohol. Often the Trappist ales are fermented at higher than normal temperatures for an ale yeast which increases the array of complex flavors from the yeast.

For hops, noble hop varieties or Styrian Goldings hops are commonly used. Occasionally low alpha English hops may also be added. Despite the hop rate of Tripel needed to balance the malt, hops is not a major flavor in either finished beer style. Large amounts of finishing and dry hops are not typically used for this beer for the same reason.

Water used for brewing is usually soft – without a large quantity of hard minerals present. Both styles are traditionally bottle conditioned with medium to high carbonation which adds to the beer's presentation.

Mashing is done with a medium to full bodied mash profile, as Trappist beers are full bodied.

Trappist ales provide a unique challenge to the home brewer – but dive in and give a Trappist a try! It is a very enjoyable style to brew.

German Kolsch

You want a good lager, but you can't make one because you do not have refrigeration? Try a making a Kölschbier! This article and recipe was graciously provided by my friend DJ Speiss of **fermentarium.com**

History

Kölsch (pronounced "koelsch") is a beer brewed exclusively by the breweries in Köln (or Cologne to the English speaking countries). The beer style has been around for several centuries, but was never called Kölsch until the Sünner brewery labeled it as such in 1918. In the 1930s, at least 40 breweries made Kölsch. Unfortunately the World War decimated the German Kölsch industry and only 2 breweries remained.

Since the European Union gave special protection to Kölsch in 1997 (geschützte Herkunftsbezeichnung), only 14 breweries legally produce Kölsch. This restriction is an extension of the Kölsch Convention of 1986. The Kölsch Convention states that Kölsch must be brewed in Köln, pale in color, top-fermented (ale), hop accentuated, and filtered. In short, the beer is a pale ale from Köln.

The culture of this beer is also unique. People from all economic classes enjoy the beer. Karl Marx remarked that his revolution could never take hold in Köln, because the workers drink with their bosses. The breweries all agreed that no Kölsch would be sold with "special", "extra" or any other add-on names.

But it tastes like a lager!

Kölsch is ale that tastes like a lager. If you handed a Kölsch to an unaware beer drinker, it is very common to mistake the beer as a lager. The beer has a very soft mouthfeel. It can be slightly sweet, but has no malty aroma and finishes very dry. Some Kölschbiers have some fruity flavor, but it is very slight. Any fruitiness in the beer should be very subtle.

There is no hop aroma and little hop flavor. It is very low in esters, and has no diacetyl. These beers typically are between 4% to 4.5% ABV. The Brewer Style guidelines list the beer's alcohol content at 4.4 – 5.2% ABV, but I would error on the lower end of the spectrum. The color of the beer is straw-like (3.5-7 SRM). Kölsch is similar to an American Blonde Ale, but finishes much cleaner and crisper.

Some commercial examples of the beer are Reissdorf, Gaffel, Alaska Summer Ale, Harpoon Summer Beer, or Sünner Kölsch. The American versions are "Kölsch-style" since they cannot be called "Kölsch".

The Recipe

Like any German beer, the ingredients for this beer follow the German purity law: Reinheitsgebot. Kölsch typically uses German pilsner malt and/or pale malt. Some recipes use wheat malt or Vienna malt, but it is less common. Wheat malt is not common in the commercial versions of the beer, but shows up in many homebrew recipes. Most Kölsch recipes use Spalt hops, but other German noble hops can be used. The beer uses very soft water and is often lagered for a month after fermentation. Here's the recipe I use.

- 10 lbs (4.5 kg) German Pilsner Malt
- 0.5 lbs (0.23 kg) German Munich Malt
- 1.5 oz (42 g) Spalt hops (4% AA bittering for 60 minutes)
- White Labs WLP029 German Ale/ Kölsch or Wyeast 2565 Kölsch

If you are an extract brewer, use 8 lbs (3.6 kg) of Pilsner LME and 0.25 lbs (0.11 kg) of Munich LME. Sometimes Spalt hops are difficult to find. You can substitute with Saaz, Hallertau, or Tettnanger. Mt. Hood can also be used. The hop you select is strictly for bittering, because Kölsch should have little to no hop flavor and no hop aroma.

Mash the grain for 90 minutes at 150°F (65°C). This should give you a good fermentable wort. Boil the wort for 90 minutes. At the 60 minute mark, add your hops.

Ferment the beer at 60°F (15°C) or as close as you can get to 60°F (15°C). Once the fermentation is complete, find a cold place to store the beer for a few weeks. A lagering period will help the beer if you can do it, but don't sweat it if you can't.

At bottling, add 1 ¼ cup of light DME that is boiled in 2 cups of water for 10 minutes. If you are kegging, carbonate the beer to 2.5 volumes.

This beer is great for those hot summer days. I've even heard it referred to as the "lawnmower ale". The traditional serving glass for Kölsch is a cylindrical 200 ml glass called a stange (pole). The serving temperature should be cellar temperatures (50°F/10°C).

Weizen and Weisse Wheat Beer Styles

Wheat, Weizen and Weisse beer recipes have become very popular craft and homebrew beer styles here in the United States over the last 20 years. In this section, we'll look at the history of wheat beer, how to brew a wheat beer and a sampling of wheat beer recipes including both Bavarian Weissebier and Berliner Weisse.

Wheat Beer History

Since wheat is a staple grain, it should be no surprise that wheat has been used for several thousand years to brew beer. There is historical evidence to suggest that wheat has been used in brewing much longer than barley, and in fact barley beer became popular only in the last few hundred years. Daniels, in <u>Designing Great Beers</u>, mentions that in certain historical periods the use of wheat for brewing was actually banned over concerns that too much wheat was being diverted from the food supply to making beer.

Modern wheat beer is centered around two German styles: the more popular Bavarian Weissebier from southern Germany and Berliner Weisse from Berlin. American wheat beer is similar in many ways to Bavarian Weisse, but without the characteristic Bavarian wheat yeast.

German brewing literature contains many references to wheat beer going back at least to the 1400's in areas spanning from Denmark to Hamburg to Vienna.

Bavarian Weisse (white beer) has a much more direct lineage. According to Ray Daniels, the first wheat beers were brewed under noble license of the Degenberger clan in the 15th century. In that same period, the first wheat beer brewery was built in Munich, and the brewing of Weissebier was strictly controlled and licensed by various dukes throughout the 16th-18th centuries. In 1872, royal control was finally loosened to move weisse brewing rights into the public domain.

Wheat Beer Brewing
Wheat lacks a few key nutrients and enzymes needed for proper conversion of sugars during mashing, so malted wheat is always combined with barley malt to provide enzymes for mashing and fermentation, often at a mix of between 40 and 60% wheat. Bavarian wheat beer derives the distinct clove and banana flavor from the use of distinct strains of yeast. Similarly Berliner Weisse uses a distinct yeast strain along with lactic acid bacteria to produce a tart flavor. American wheat beer has a more neutral flavor from the use of common ale yeast.

German wheat beers were traditionally brewed using decoction methods, though a home brewer can achieve excellent results with a single step infusion mash. Fermentation temperatures are very important in wheat beer due to the sensitivity of the yeasts involved. I recommend a fermentation temperature of 64-66 F (around 18C).

Bavarian Weisse or Weizen
Weisse has a target original gravity of 1.040 to 1.056, color of 2 to 9 SRM, and bitterness between 10 and 20 IBUs. It has

very low bitterness, low to medium body and high esters as well as banana and clove flavor derived from the yeast.

Bavarian Weisse or Weizen is almost always made from only two base malts: wheat malt and pilsner or pale malt. The percentage of wheat malt varies from as little as 20% to as much as 60%, but 40-50% is a good average number. Note that wheat malt can't be steeped and must be mashed, so if you are an extract brewer be sure to use wheat or weizen extract as the base malt. Decoction or a single infusion mash is acceptable with a recommended conversion temperature of around 152F/67C.

The hop schedule for Weisse is minimal – a single noble hop addition at the beginning of the boil. Hallertau hops are most commonly used, though Saaz, Tettnanger and Hersbrucker are also popular. A low hop rate giving 15-17 IBUs is typical. The use of distinctive Bavarian wheat yeast is critical to the style, as so much of the Bavarian flavor profile is derived from the yeast itself.

Bavarian Weisse is highly carbonated, at 2.4-3.0 volumes. Hefeweizen (with yeast) is served relatively young with the yeast still in suspension giving a cloudy character. Krystal (clear) is filtered commercially to give a crystal clear finish.

American Wheat Beer

American wheat beer shares much in common with Bavarian Weisse, using basically the same grain bill, low hop rate, and pale color. The main difference is that American wheat beer is typically fermented with American ale yeast, giving a neutral and clean finish, but lacking the banana and clove flavor that Bavarian wheat yeast provides. American wheat beer is often served at moderate carbonation and occasionally uses American hops, though hop flavoring is not significant for the style.

Berliner Weisse

Berliner Weisse has an original gravity between 1.026 and 1.036, a very low hop rate of 3-8 IBUs, a pale color between 2-4 SRM and is served highly carbonated (2.5-3.0 volumes). The flavor profile is sour from the use of lactic bacteria or lactic acid. They have a light body, and dry tart finish.

Berliner Weisse is typically brewed from equal parts of wheat and pilsner or pale malt base, though in some cases up to 70% wheat may be used. Extract brewers should use a base of weizen or wheat extract. Low hop rates are used in a single hop addition, and again noble hops such as Hallertau, Saaz or Tettnanger are most popular.

Berliner yeast is most often used with the addition of either lactic acid bacteria after primary fermentation. As an alternative, some home brewers spike their beer with food grade lactic acid (Daniel's recommends 90 ml for 7 gallons) to give the sour, lactic finish required.

Wheat beers of any type are refreshing, smooth and light and are great beers to have in stock year round.

Marzen and Oktoberfest Beer

The German Marzen and Oktoberfest beer styles are seasonal favorites of beer drinkers worldwide. In this section we take a look at the traditional Marzen and Oktoberfest beer recipes and how to brew them at home.

Marzen has a mixed origin. Some sources note the extremely close relationship between Marzen and Vienna beers. Ray Daniels notes that the term Marzen was first used for beers brewed in Vienna in the 1700's. Marzen is also close in relation to brown beers brewed in Bavaria as early as the 16th century, though the term Marzen was not originally applied to this style. Most modern authors attribute the origin of the name "Marzen" to Vienna, as no references can be found of

Munich Marzen's prior to the late 19th century, though similar styles were being brewed in Bavaria much earlier.

Marzen, the German word for the month of March, refers to the month in which these beers were originally brewed. Summer was too hot to brew and ferment beers properly, so by a 1539 ordinance in Bavaria, beer could only be brewed between the days of St Michael and Saint George (29 Sept-23 April).

As beer was not brewed in the summer, the last beers of spring were made with a higher alcohol content and stored in cellars, often refrigerated with ice to last the summer. This higher gravity beer was named after the month – March or Marzen.

The modern Marzen and Oktoberfest styles may bear little resemblance to the early Marzen of Vienna or even Munich. The early Marzen was described as dark, brown and full bodied. In fact, the turmoil of the wars of the early 20th century Europe nearly brought an end to both Marzen and Vienna style beers, though the modern Marzen enjoyed a resurgence in popularity when the Munich Oktoberfest started up again after World War II. The Oktoberfest style, a slightly stronger version of Marzen, is brewed specifically for the world famous Munich festival each year.

The Marzen Beer Style

The BJCP style guide describes Marzen as a rich, slightly malty beer with a hint of toasted character from Vienna malt. No roasted or caramel flavors are present, and the beer has a fairly dry finish. Noble hops are present though should be only lightly perceived in the finished beer which is decidedly malty.

The original gravity of a Marzen is in the 1.050-1.057 range, lightly bittered with noble hops providing 20-28 IBUs of bitterness. Some "fest" beers are brewed at a slightly higher starting gravity. The beer is well attenuated, with a finishing gravity of 1.012-1.016. Color should be golden to orange-amber with a color range of 7-14 SRM. The alcohol by volume is 4.8%-5.7% and Marzen's are usually fairly well carbonated.

Brewing a Marzen Recipe

Marzen is made from a combination of Munich, 2-row Pale Malt, Pilsner and Vienna malts. The malty Munich malts makes up as much as half of the grain bill, with either Pilsner or Pale Malt making the balance of the grain bill. For extract recipes, a Munich based extract made from Munich and Pale malt is generally best to use as a base. Vienna may be added to substitute for 10-15% of the Munich malt to add a slightly more toasted flavor. A small number of homebrew recipes also add 5-10% Crystal or 5% Cara-pils malt to add body and head retention.

Hops for Marzen/Oktoberfest beers is typically of the Noble German or Bohemian variety, and the bitterness ratio (BU:GU) is generally around 0.5-0.6. Popular hops selections include Saaz, Tettnanger, and Hallertauer though occasionally American hops are used by homebrewers. These are added for bittering, and aroma or dry hops are rarely used.

The mash is typically a single infusion mash for homebrewers in the middle range of around 152-154F (67-68C) for the conversion step. Purists can try a traditional German decoction mash, though in most cases it is unnecessary given modern highly modified malts.

Bavarian lager yeast or Marzen/Oktoberfest yeast is the prime choice for Marzens, with Bohemian Pilsner yeast providing a reasonable backup. Ferment at around 50F/10C (depending on yeast choice) and lager near freezing (33-37F or 1-3C) for at least 5 weeks.

Water treatments are rarely needed, but you might want to consider alternative water sources if your water is exceptionally hard.

Marzen and Oktoberfest is an enjoyable malty brew, especially for the fall season. Plan ahead and brew some next fall.

Bock and Doppelbock Beers

Bock beer is a classic German lager that is smooth and very drinkable. Traditionally bock was brewed in winter. In this section we look at how to brew the classic Bock beer style.

History of Bock

Bock traces its origins back to the town of Einbeck in Northern Germany as early as 1325. The beer of Einbeck was not only popular but widely distributed to Hamburg and Bremen. Lightly kilned wheat and barley was used in the original Einbeck beer, which had only a remote similarity to the modern bock style. Wheat was used for approximately 1/3 of the grain bill, and barley malt made up the rest.

Alas, Einbeck was ravaged by two fires in the 16th century and then suffered greatly in the 30 years war (1618-1648), so little of the original style survives. In the 16th century, Munich tried to emulate the great beers of Einbeck and started brewing variants that were called "Ainpoeckish Pier", named in the Bavarian dialect for the city of Einbeck.

Later, the name was shortened to "Poeck" and ultimately "Bock", which means "Goat" in German. In the 1800's bock enjoyed a resurgence as brewing techniques and science improved. The addition of the hydrometer and thermometer, controlled lagering and other techniques helped dramatically. Bock then spread well beyond Munich to Vienna and throughout Germany.

German immigrants brought Bock to America in the late 1800's where it, along with Pilsner became popular. Best & Company (later Pabst) became one of the first to brew it broadly in America. Bock, traditionally quite strong in Europe, was brewed at lower strength after Prohibition in America.

Variants of the bock style include Doppelbock, Maibock, Eisbock, American bock and Weizenbock. Doppelbock means, "double bock" and is brewed with a minimum original gravity of 1.074, which is slightly stronger than traditional bock and typically has complex chocolate and caramel flavoring. Maibock, or "May bock" is tapped in the Spring and has a much paler color than traditional bock, and is made from a mixture of Munich and Pilsner malts.

Eisbock, or "Ice bock" which has a minimum OG of 1.093 is a very strong bock that is highly alcoholic and malty. Though made in the tradition of regular bock and Doppelbock, the strength of the beer approaches that of some barley wines. American bock is made primarily in the Midwest and Texas, and is typically somewhat lighter in gravity than traditional German bock and may be a bit less malty in flavor. Weizenbock is perhaps better characterized as a Dunkel-Weizen brewed to bock or Doppelbock strength, and not technically a bock beer. It is composed primarily of around 60% malted wheat with Munich or Vienna malt filling the rest of the grain bill, and fermented with wheat yeast rather than lager yeast.

The Bock Style

The modern bock style closely tracks the traditional German style of the last hundred years. Bock has a fairly strong original gravity of 1.064-1.072 and a dark amber to brown color between 14 and 22 SRM. German bocks must have a minimum starting gravity of 1.064. The flavor of the beer is malty with a slight chocolate or toasted edge. Bocks have medium to full bodied profiles, but no roast flavor.

The carbonation is moderate, and hop flavor is minimal. Typically German hops are used to balance some of the maltiness of the beer with an IBU level of 20-27 IBUs. Lager yeast is used along with cold temperature storage (lagering) at temperatures near freezing.

Brewing a Bock

Munich malt makes up the bulk of the grain bill for any Bock. In fact, most traditional Bocks are made from a single Munich malt, with variations in kilning determining the color and character of the finished beer. Daniels recommends using Munich malt for 75-93% of the grist, with pale or lager malt making up the balance. For all grain brewers, this is your best route to an authentic bock. Where possible, choose a two row Munich malt as the base.

Analysis of many award winning homebrewed recipes indicates that crystal and chocolate are often added – especially for the dunkel (dark) bock varieties. Crystal makes up 10-15% of the grain bill and chocolate approximately 2% – primarily to add color.

For extract brewers, try to secure a Munich based malt extract if possible, as it is difficult to achieve the proper malty balance without it. Extract recipes often use some crystal or chocolate malt to achieve the appropriate color and body, but these should be used sparingly. If you are brewing a partial mash recipe, the addition of Munich and pale malt will add authenticity to the recipe.

Not surprisingly, German hops are used extensively in Bock. Hallertauer hops are the traditional choice for bock, though Tettnanger, Hersbruck or Saaz are occasionally used. Do not use high alpha hops in a bock as it will upset the malty balance. Bock is not a hoppy beer, so the bulk of hop additions are used during the boil for bitterness. Small flavor or aroma additions are OK, but hop flavor and aroma is not a dominant feature in this beer.

The traditional mash schedule for a German bock is a triple decoction, though with modern highly modified grains a double decoction will suffice. Decoction does help to enhance the color and body of the beer to bring out the strong malty profile of a traditional bock. The protein rest should target around 122F/50C, while the main conversion should be done at a slightly higher temperature of 155-156 F (68C) to bring out the desired medium to full body beer profile. A single infusion mash is also an option, again in the 155F/68C range.

Munich water profiles have a high proportion of carbonate, which is why hops are sparingly used to avoid harsh bitterness. However, most domestic brewing waters can produce a good bock style since the darker bock malts help provide the proper mash pH balance, and adding carbonate really does not enhance this particular style.

Munich/Bavarian lager yeast should be used for your bock recipe. Cold lagering during fermentation and storage is critical. The fermentation temperature should match the recommended range for your yeast, but fermentation is usually done around 50F/10C. Once fermentation is complete, the actual lagering should take place close to freezing, and continue for 4-10 weeks as these lager yeasts often take some time to flocculate (sediment).

Bocks are wonderful beers to brew year round, especially if you have a temperature controlled fermenter to lager your bock.

German Altbier

German Altbier or Alt is a top fermenting beer that originated in the German Westphalia region and later grew in popularity around the Rhineland. Here, we take a look at brewing Altbier at home. The term "Alt" or "old beer" refers to the old methods of using a top fermenting ale yeast at ale temperatures but then cold aging the beer to form a slightly bitter, malty, well attenuated German ale. The term Altbier first appeared in the 1800's to differentiate this traditional ale from newer pale lagers then becoming popular in Germany.

The BJCP recognizes two distinct style of Altbier; the Dusseldorf Alt is primarily produced near the town of Dusseldorf, and is slightly more bitter than the more widely brewed Northern German Altbier. The Northern version generally has a slight caramel flavor and is sweeter and less bitter than the Dusseldorf. Some Altbiers are also produced in small quantities in the Netherlands near the German border as well as Austria, Switzerland and the US microbreweries.

The Altbier Style

Altbier is an amber colored ale with a very smooth, well attenuated finish. The beer should be well balanced with some bitterness and some maltiness. Fruitiness from the ale yeast is appropriate. Color is generally bronze to brown (11-17 SRM). There is low dyacetyl flavor and the beer generally has moderate to high carbonation.

There are differences between the Northern and Dusseldorf Altbier styles. The Dusseldorf style has medium bitterness and medium to high maltiness and is often brewed with moderately carbonate water. The Northen style may have a malty, grainy, biscuity and even slight caramel maltiness. The Northern style is generally less bitter than the Dusseldorf and is sometimes made with a mix of ale and lager yeasts or even a highly attentive lager yeast alone.

The BJCP style guide specifies an original gravity of 1.046-1.054 and final gravity of 1.010-1.015 for both styles. The Dusseldorf color runs bronze to brown, or 11-17 SRM. The Northern can be slightly darker at 13-19 SRM. Carbonation is a bubbly 2.5-3.1 volumes of CO_2.

Brewing an Altbier

The base malt for Alt is German Pilsner malt, which typically makes up 80% of the grain bill. A small amount of Munich or Vienna malt is often used to add some malty flavor. Dark Crystal malt is used in the Northern style to reach the appropriate color and add a small bit of caramel flavor. The Dusseldorf style uses less crystal malt, and instead substitutes small amounts of chocolate or black malt to achieve the desired color.

The traditional mash schedule is a German triple decoction, though a single step infusion mash is more than adequate if you are using modern highly modified malt.

Both styles require a highly attentive yeast with a clean finish. The Dusseldorf style always uses a high attenuation ale yeast such as White Labs WLP036 Dusseldorf Alt Yeast or WLP001 California Ale or Wyeast 1056 American Ale. The Northern Alt style also requires a high attenuation yeast, and most often lager yeasts are used though occasionally a mix of ale/lager or ale yeast may be used. Interesting yeasts to use include various German Lager yeasts, Kolsch yeasts from both labs, and the Alt ale yeasts listed above.

Spalt hops are traditionally used for the Dusseldorf alt, though many noble hop varieties are suitable as well. The Northern style uses noble hop varieties as well and there is some variation between breweries on which is best to use. The Dusseldorf style may use moderately carbonate water to accentuate the bitterness of the hops while the Northern style typically does not use carbonate water.

Altbier is one of my favorite continental styles to brew. It has a distinctive malty flavor that sets it apart from English ales.

Chapter 11: American Beer Styles

*"Beer is proof that God loves us and wants
us to be happy"*

– Benjamin Franklin

While American beer styles are sometimes derided as imitations of popular English and European styles made with American ingredients, the truth is that the US has created some truly unique beer styles. While the US once had a diverse and innovative beer market, it was largely wiped out by prohibition and World War. However, in the last 25 years we've enjoyed a resurgence of the craft beer and microbrew industry, once again providing us with innovative brews of all kinds.

American Amber Ale

American Amber Ale, also known in the Pacific Northwest as Red Ale is a uniquely American beer that is robust, rich and enjoyable. A fairly recent style, Ambers have become very popular with mainstream beer drinkers in the US. In this section we take a look at the American Amber style, how to brew it at home and some examples of American Amber recipes.

American Amber became popular in the Pacific Northwest before spreading nationwide, primarily through microbreweries and small regional brewers. These beers are also called Red Ales or West Coast Ales in some regions, but the style itself overlaps somewhat with American Pale Ale. Amber ales have a stronger caramel flavor, more body, are darker and color and have a balance between bitterness and maltiness, where Pale

Ales tend to have a stronger hop flavor. Amber ale is also popular in Australia, with the most popular being from Malt Shovel Brewery (James Squire Amber).

The American Amber Ale Style

The Amber style is considered somewhat richer than pale ale, and is recognized by the Beer Judge Certification Program (BJCP) as its own style (10-B). Ambers can have moderate to high hop flavor, but the hops should not be dominant. American hops are most often use which can result in a somewhat citrusy flavor. Malt sweetness and a caramel flavor are desirable, but Amber should not have the roasted character of a brown ale. Few esters and no dicetyl are desirable.

Stronger versions may have some alcohol warmth, but the finish should be smooth. Medium to full body for the beer is normal, with moderate to high carbonation. The BJCP specifies an original gravity of 1.045-1.060 and final gravity of 1.010-1.015 giving 4.5-6.2% alcohol by volume.

Bitterness is between 25-40 IBUs, giving an average bitterness ratio of 0.619 BU/GU which places amber ales slightly on the malty side as far as overall balance. Color is amber to copper brown, with an SRM of 10-17, though some mass produced ambers run at the low end of the color range.

Ambers are moderate to highly carbonated, and typically have good head retention.

Brewing an Amber Ale

Amber Ale is made with American two row pale malt as the base, making up 60-85% of the grain bill. Medium to dark crystal malts are used to provide color and caramel flavor, typically making up 10-20% of the grain bill. Small amounts of other specialty grains such as a tiny amount of roast malt (for red color versions), aromatic malt, carafoam, munich or victory malts may be used to add unique character to the brew.

There is no fixed water profile associated with Amber ale, so a variety of waters can be used. However, as the water does not add significantly to the flavor for this style, a moderate water profile (not too high in sulfates or carbonates) is desirable.

American hops are traditionally used, with citrus varieties such as centennial being popular. Like pale ale, it is not unusual to use multiple hop additions during the boil as well as a moderate amount of fresh dry hops to provide some hoppy aroma, though overall the beer should be well balanced, with the balance slightly to the malty side.

As a full body Amber is desirable, one generally uses a full bodied single step infusion mash with the conversion step at 156-158F (69-70C) for approximately 45 minutes to an hour. Since the beer is generally 100% barley malt, no special techniques are needed.

Most amber ales are fermented with American ale yeast, which provides a fairly clean finish with high attenuation. Some of the more robust and rich Ambers may also feature use of lighter English ale yeasts that can contribute low to moderate esters and complexity to the beer without unbalancing it. Ambers are fermented and aged at normal ale temperatures (64-68F or 18-20C), and should be bottled or kegged with moderate to medium-high carbonation.

American Amber is an example of the unique character of new American beer styles. I hope you enjoy an American Amber soon!

American Cream Ale

Cream Ale is a distinctly American beer style that is refreshing and smooth. It has enjoyed a resurgence recently as many microbreweries have taken up the style and even improved upon commercial versions.

Cream ale enjoyed broad popularity in the pre-prohibition era, and was particularly popular in the Midwest. The distinct style emerged in the latter half of the 19th century as a variation of increasingly popular pilsners. A darker, slightly sour variation called Dark Cream Common or Common Beer was brewed in the area surrounding Louisville Kentucky.

In the UK, the term "cream ale" is also used to describe nitrogen-dispensed beers that have a rich creamy head, though these ales bear little relation to the American style. The term "smooth ale" is now more commonly used to describe these English beers.

The Cream Ale Style

Cream ale is essentially an ale brewed with lager yeast at warm ale temperatures, much like its California cousin, Steam Beer. The beer is brewed from American 6 row barley usually with corn adjuncts.

The flavor profile of a cream ale has a hint of malt, along with a sweet corn-like aroma. A hint of DMS is common due to the use of lager yeast. The hop and malt should be balanced with neither dominating. They generally have a crisp body with a clean finish.

Starting gravities are in the medium 1.042-1.055 range, and color ranges from pale to moderate gold color (2-5 SRM). Bitterness is subtle but balanced, in the 15-20+ IBU range. Cream ales are served refrigerated and highly carbonated.

Brewing a Cream Ale

The bulk of the grain bill (80%) for any cream ale is American malt, usually 6 row pale barley malt, though sometimes 2 row is used. Corn adjuncts such as flaked maize may be used for up to 20% of the grain bill. Corn based sugars in the boil are also commonly added in the place of corn. Other adjuncts are less common, but some recipes use carafoam or very light caramel malt to add body.

American hops should be used, but it is wise to avoid high alpha modern hops that can unbalance the pale malt flavor. Noble hops are also acceptable. The normal hop schedule uses both boil and finishing hop additions to add to the flavor profile and aroma.

The choice of yeast and control of fermentation temperature is perhaps most important to this style. Some modern brewers use a mix of ale and lager yeast strains, though historically just lager yeast was used. American lager strains mixed with an American ale strain work best.

Fermentation temperatures should be controlled, though fermentation is done well above normal lager temperature ranges. Fermentation in the 65-68F (18-20C) range provides a reasonable balance without excess ester production from the lager yeast.

Many modern cream ales are cold lagered to enhance clarity and flavor, though historically cream ales were not lagered in this way. If you do lager, I recommend keeping the beer at cold temperatures (around 40F/4.5C) for several weeks once your beer has completely fermented and has carbonated.

Cream ale is designed as a cold refreshing drink on a hot day, so it should be served cold and well carbonated (2.6-3.2 vols) much like a lager beer. Consider brewing a Cream Ale as your next beer.

Steam Beer and California Common

Steam Beer brings to mind visions of the California gold rush, the Sierra Nevada Mountains, and San Francisco. Here we'll look at the history of California common beer (aka Steam

Beer) and how to design steam beer recipes and present a collection of Steam Beer recipes you can brew at home.

History of Steam Beer

Steam beer was originally made by dozens of breweries in the California from 1850-1920, particularly around San Francisco. After prohibition, Anchor Steam Brewing Company continued to brew steam beer and eventually trademarked the term "Steam Beer" for use with its famous brew. Since "Steam Beer" was trademarked by Anchor Brewing Company, brewers adopted the name "California Common" to refer to this unique beer style.

The key distinguishing feature of steam beer is that it is a lager beer fermented at high temperatures (between 60-65F or 15-18C) and often well hopped. The precise origin of California Steam Beer is somewhat ambiguous. Ray Daniels in <u>Designing Great Beers</u> notes that "One Hundred Years of Brewing" provides conflicting information on precisely where the first steam beer was made (Los Angeles and San Francisco being candidates), but says that at least 25 California breweries made steam beer in the period from 1850-1903. The origins of the term "steam beer" are also shrouded in mystery, but one source cites the escaping gas when a keg of steam beer was tapped.

Anchor Brewing started making steam beer in 1894 and was the sole producer of the beer through the 1960's after prohibition closed its competitors. The original steam beer was cask fermented and conditioned, and often delivered to the saloon in a "young" state.

The historic version may or may not have used adjuncts, was hopped between 28 and 40 IBUs, and was run through a "clarifier" after a very short fermentation directly into the keg. Krausen was used to carbonate the kegs, often to very high levels of carbonation (as high as 40-70 psi before tapping!).

Designing a California Common Recipe

The modern California Common beer remains remarkably true to the steam beer heritage. California Common has an original gravity between 1.048 and 1.054, and a moderate hopping level of 30-45 IBUs according to the BJCP Style Guide.

It is brewed with a medium body, and the distinct flavor of Northern Brewer hops. It is typically amber to light copper in color, between 10 and 14 SRM. The modern beer is more highly attenuated than its predecessor, and has a mix of ale and lager character. This leaves a clean finish with low fruitiness, ester and diacytl.

California Common uses a pale malt (usually 2 row or pale extract) base for the bulk of the malt bill. Crystal malt in the 40-80L color range makes up an average of 10% of the remaining malt bill and is selected to achieve the desired beer color. Additional ingredients such as Munich/Vienna, Cara Pils, Chocolate and Special malts are occasionally added to homebrew versions, usually in quantities of 5% or less.

The mash schedule should target 152-156F (67-69C) to produce a medium body beer. Hop aroma and bitterness are desirable for this style, so multiple hop additions are the norm. Northern Brewer hops are traditionally used for bittering with an aroma hops such as Cascade added near the end of the boil for flavor/aroma. Dry hopping is often used. The water used historically for this beer is soft in character.

A distinguishing feature of California Common is clearly its fermentation and yeast strain. California Common lager yeast is most often used, though many brewers have had great success with high attenuation lager yeasts or even high attenuation ale yeast. Steam beer should be fermented between 60-68 F (16-20C). Conditioning homebrew at 50F/10C for 3-4 weeks after fermentation will aid in clearing the beer.

Chapter 12: Bonus Articles

*"I would give all my fame for a pot of ale
and safety"*

– Henry V, Shakespeare

Here are a few bonus articles from the BeerSmith blog that did not fit in elsewhere in the book, but I thought you might enjoy. I've included two articles on choosing equipment that have been hot topics on many discussion forums – these being the eternal debate of glass vs. plastic fermenters and aluminum vs. stainless steel pots.

Finally, I finish with two summaries of tips which are partially covered in other articles, but still have been very popular on the BeerSmith blog.

Glass vs. Plastic Fermenters – Which is Better?

One perpetual debate among home brewers is the relative advantages of glass vs plastic fermenting vessels for making beer. Most beginner home brew kits come with a large plastic pail with a plastic top. However, many advanced brewers swear by the advantages of the classic 5 gallon glass carboy. So, who is right? In this section we take a look at them side by side.

The Plastic Fermentation Vessel (aka Bucket)

Most brewers start fermenting in a 5 gallon food grade plastic bucket. These buckets are cheap, durable and relatively easy to clean. However, the plastic bucket has both advantages and disadvantages:

- The plastic bucket is easy to clean – since the entire top comes off, you can reach in and scrub any grime off in a few minutes
- Plastic is durable – if you do drop the bucket it is unlikely it will break
- Plastic is harder to sanitize completely – over time it does get small scratches on the inside which can be a haven for bacteria and germs, which is why most brewers recommend replacing plastic buckets after a year or two
- Plastic is not suitable for long term storage of beer (i.e. months), as it is permeable to air
- Many plastic buckets have a poor seal between the bucket and cover – which can result in air being introduced as well as the brewer thinking fermentation is done prematurely (as the airlock has stopped bubbling due to the leaks)

The Glass Carboy

In the other corner, we have the 5 gallon glass carboy. A carboy is a large water bottle made of real glass, and usually comes in either a 5 gallon or 6.5 gallon size. Glass carboys are obviously far less durable, but are the favorite of many advanced brewers. Some advantages/disadvantages include:

- Impermeable to Air – Air cannot penetrate the glass, so you can leave your fermented beer in a glass carboy for months without worrying about it being spoiled by air (oxidation). Also you don't have to worry about leaks through the top as a proper stopper and airlock will form an air-tight seal.
- Easy to Sanitize – Glass will not pit or scratch like plastic, so you don't have to worry about scratches creating havens for bacteria. Further, as the glass is transparent it is pretty easy to see if it is completely clean.
- You can Watch Your Brew – While not a huge deal, many brewers like being able to see the beer as it is fermenting to get an idea of the size of the Krausen layer, how active the fermentation is and how much sediment has formed.

- Harder to Clean – After fermentation is complete and you have transferred or bottled your beer, it can be harder to clean a glass carboy than a plastic bucket. You need a large bottle brush to do it properly and even then you may find some areas are more difficult to reach with the brush than others.
- Easy to Break – I've broken at least three carboys inadvertently, though thankfully I have not yet broken a full one. However, carboys are difficult to lift and maneuver, and will shatter if you bump them against any solid surface. Breaking a full carboy can be a major safety hazard as well as a huge mess. Some brewers have been seriously injured by breaking carboys. I try to arrange my brewing setup so I move my carboys as little as possible once they are full.
- More Expensive – Carboys are more expensive than plastic fermentation buckets, and you also need to consider that you may break a few during your brewing career.

A Third Alternative: The Modern Plastic Carboy

A modern alternative that mixes some of the advantages of the glass carboy and the plastic bucket is to use special plastic carboys. These are typically made of a lightweight food grade plastic intended to be largely impermeable to oxygen and non-absorbing. The most popular manufacturer of these is a company called Better Bottle®.

Some of the advantages and disadvantages include:

- Almost Impermeable to Air and Beer – While not as impermeable as pure glass, these special plastics do a good job of keeping air out so you can ferment your beer for an extended period if needed.
- Light Weight and Hard to Break – These plastic carboys are largely shatter-proof so you don't need to worry about them breaking if dropped.

- Moderately Easy to Clean and Sanitize – Though you should not use a brush on these plastic carboys, they do usually come clean with a good soaking. Since they are clear in color you easily spot any dirt.
- More Expensive – These carboys are more expensive than a plastic bucket but run about the same price as a glass carboy. Given the risk of breakage with glass, a plastic carboy may outlast a glass one.

The Bottom Line

So which is best? I personally use glass carboys for both stages of my fermentation, and have for the last 15+ years. However, I am thinking seriously of purchasing a modern plastic carboy for my next fermenter as I would like to avoid the nightmare scenario of 5 gallons of beer in a carboy breaking over my feet. However, the choice, as always, is yours!

Aluminum vs. Stainless Steel Brewing Pots – Which is Better?

Another debate among home brewers are the merits of aluminum vs stainless steel pots for brewing beer. In this section, we look at the pros and cons of each to help you make your own educated decision on your next beer brewing pot.

Aluminum Pot Pros and Cons

Aluminum pots are widely available and inexpensive because aluminum cookware is used worldwide for preparing foods. Inexpensive Turkey pots in the 36 quart range can be found at your local department store, particularly right after Thanksgiving at great prices. Aluminum pots cost considerably less than stainless steel – often half as much. Aluminum is a better conductor of heat than steel, so your pot will come to a boil faster and also cool down faster after you are done boiling.

The only major disadvantage of aluminum is that it will oxidize, so you can't use oxygen-based or caustic cleaners such as OxyClean. This is the major reason why professional brewing equipment is made of stainless steel and not aluminum – the stainless steel is easier to clean with caustic cleaning agents. Also, over time aluminum will get an oxide layer over it which can discolor the aluminum and give it a grey tone. This is not a cause for concern – the layer of aluminum oxide actually protects the pot, but it is not as pretty as stainless steel.

I feel it is important to address a number of myths about aluminum. First, aluminum pots are not linked to Alzheimer's disease. A number of medical studies since the 1970's have found zero link between Alzheimer's and the use of aluminum. Keep in mind that every day you eat food prepared in aluminum cookware – it is safe.

A second myth is that aluminum will react with acidic content of the wort and either add off flavors or eat away at your pot. This is also untrue – water has a pH of 7.0, your wort has a pH of around 5.2, while spaghetti sauce can run as low as 4.6 and the most acidic diet sodas you drink run as low as 2.5. For comparison, battery acid has a pH of 1.0. Your wort is simply not acidic enough to react with your aluminum pot.

Stainless Steel

Stainless steel pots are the "Cadillac" of brewing pots, with designer pots running into the many hundreds of dollars in price. They are more expensive than comparable aluminum pots, but are a favorite of serious brewers. Stainless steel will remain shiny, as the passive oxide layer is not visible – so it's easy to tell when your stainless pot is truly clean.

An advantage of stainless steel is that you can use oxygenated cleaners on it, which makes it a clear choice with professional brewers who need to clean large vats. You should avoid long term exposure to bleach based cleaners as these can pit your stainless steel pots and vessels.

Stainless steel is stronger than the softer aluminum metal, so it is less prone to denting and scratching for a comparable wall thickness. However, you are unlikely to outlive a well made stainless or aluminum pot in either case. Stainless has a strongly bonded oxide layer, so it is less susceptible to attack by acids, though again the acidity of wort is not a concern for either metal.

The major disadvantage of stainless steel is that it does not conduct heat as well as aluminum, which means a longer time to reach boil and also longer cooling times after the boil.

Which to Choose?

If you select a well made heavy-duty pot, large enough for a full boils and conducts heat well, you can't go wrong with either stainless or aluminum. I look for a heavy pot with thick walls as it will conduct heat better and also hold up well to the occasional nicks and dings. An ideal pot has a diameter approximately equal to its height. A well made aluminum or stainless steel pot will likely last a lifetime.

If you are a brewer on a budget, you can't ignore the large price advantage of aluminum – often it costs half as much for a comparable pot. Stainless steel has a "cool factor", but it also has a price associated with being cool.

Ten Tips for Making Great Beer

These are the 10 things I wish I knew when I started home brewing but had to learn the hard way.

- **Keep It Sanitary** – Anything that touches your beer after it has started cooling must be sanitized using any of the popular sanitizing solutions (bleach, iodophor, etc). The period immediately after you cool your beer is particularly critical as bacteria and other infections are most likely to take hold before the yeast has started fermentation.

- **Use High Quality, Fresh Ingredients** – Fresh ingredients make better homebrew. If you started with dry yeast, move up to liquid yeast. If you are an extract brewer, look for fresh extract rather than a can that is several years old. Store liquid yeast in the refrigerator, grains in a cool dry place, and hops in the freezer. Hops, dry malt, yeast, liquid malt and crushed grains all have a limited shelf life and must be used quickly. Crushed grains, dry malt and liquid malt will oxidize over time.

- **Do your Homework** – Designing great beer is one part science and one part art. Why guess on the science part? Switching to brewing software like BeerSmith can make a difference in your brewing as it gives you the opportunity to calculate the color, bitterness and original gravity up front to match your brewing style. As I brewed more, I started reading top brewing books, engaging in discussion forums and browsing the internet for brewing resources. All of these sources, combined with experience and experimentation dramatically impacted my brewing style and consistency in a search for brewing perfection.

- **Cool the Wort Quickly** – Cooling your beer quickly will move it quickly thru the temperature range in which it would be mostly easily infected, and will dramatically increase the fallout of proteins and tannins that are bad for your beer and will also reduce the chance of infection. An immersion wort chiller is a relatively inexpensive investment that will improve the clarity and quality of your beer. Cooling is particularly important for full batch boils.

- **Boil for 60-90 Minutes** – Boiling your wort performs several important functions. It sterilizes your wort, vaporizes many undesirable compounds, releases bittering oils from the hops, and coagulates proteins and tannins from the grains so they can fall out during cooling. To achieve all of these noble goals you need to boil for at least

60 minutes, and for lighter styles of beers a longer boil of 90 minutes is desirable.

- **Control Fermentation Temperature** – Though few brewers have dedicated fermentation refrigerators, there are simple methods you can use to maintain a constant temperature for ales during fermentation. The best technique I've seen is to pick a cool, dry area in your home and then wrap the fermenter in wet towels and place a fan in front of it. Wet the towels every 12 hours or so, and you should get a steady fermentation temperature in the 66-68F range. Most brewing shops sell stick-on thermometers that can be attached to your fermentation vessel to monitor the temperature.

- **Switch to a Full Batch Boil** – Boiling all of your wort will benefit to your beer. If you are only boiling 2-3 gallons of a 5 gallon batch, then you are not getting the full benefits of a 60-90 minute boil. The purchase of a 7-12 gallon brew pot and (highly recommended) outdoor propane burner (which could make the spouse happy as you now brew outside) are great intermediate steps for moving to all-grain brewing and the full boils will improve your beer.

- **Use High Quality Fermenters** – As I covered in the last section, glass carboys. Better Bottle plastic, or stainless fermenters offer significant advantages over the typical plastic bucket.

- **Make a Yeast Starter** – While pitching directly from a tube or packet of liquid yeast is OK, your beer will ferment much better if you make a yeast starter first. Boil up a small amount of dried malt extract in 2 quarts of water with 1/4 oz (7 g) of yeast. Cool it well and then pitch your yeast into it 2-3 days before you brew. Install some foil or an airlock over it and place it in a cool dark location. When brew day comes, pitching your starter will result in a quicker start and less risk of infection or off flavors.

- **Make Long Term Purchases** – You may have started brewing with an off-the-shelf kit, but if you enjoy brewing then you are best off making long term purchases rather than a series of short term purchases. For example, early on I bought a 3 gallon pot, then a 5 gallon pot, then an 8 gallon enamel pot and finally a 9 gallon stainless. It would have been much cheaper to jump to the 9 gallon stainless after the 3 gallon pot. Similarly I've had several sizes of immersion chillers, finally settling on a two stage 3/8" diameter copper coil. If you instead make long term purchases (a good pot, a good chiller, good carboys, a nice mash tun/cooler) you will save a lot of money in the long run.

Brewing to Lose: 10 Tips for Making Bad Beer

[Authors note: This is an article I wrote just for fun for the BeerSmith blog, but many of my readers enjoyed it so I thought I would include it here for you to enjoy as well]

Anyone who has visited the trophy wing of Chateau Smith inevitably asks the tour guide the same questions. How can someone who has been brewing beer for almost a quarter of a century have so few wins? Where do you keep the big trophies? How does one consistently place last in a category with only 4 entries? Tell us the truth – how does he always manage to lose?

For a long time I merely dismissed such talk as idle chatter. Recently, however, I've come to realize that the stream of Chateau visitors were sincere – they do actually want to know how to lose. While I previously wrote about making better beer, losing is a topic that little has been written about. Yet losing is something that every brewer needs to know.

Losing is a secret desire we all aspire to. The truth is that no one likes a winner. Winners are smug, brash, and unpopular. Winners are often the target of sabotage and assassination attempts. People talk about them behind their backs.

Winners are hated, but everyone loves a loser. Losers are popular, friendly and beloved. They blend into the crowd. No one ever feels intimidated or threatened by a loser. We love to hang out with losers – after all they make us feel good about ourselves.

The good news is that every human being has within himself the innate ability to lose. Sure, any moron can produce bad beer occasionally, but I'm talking about losing on a consistent basis – year after year. That kind of losing takes dedication and effort. It requires expertise and forethought.

What you need is advice from an expert in losing. I can show you how.

We all remember our early brewing days when it was easy to make bad beer. Pitch the yeast into boiling hot wort to kill it off, throw in a few pounds of cane sugar, toss it all into our unsanitized open bucket, bottle a day or two later and voila – bad (and sometimes explosive) beer. How easy it all was back in the good old days. Losing required no effort at all.

However, over the years many of us forgot our old habits, allowed experience to creep in and lost the magic recipe for really bad beer. At first the beer became passable, then drinkable and perhaps even good. We gradually slipped from the bottom of the pack to the middle and perhaps even into the dreaded top 10%.

Fear not – for old bad habits can be relearned. With practice you can slip back out of the winner's circle into the realm of mediocrity. Without further ado, I present 10 expert tips for making award losing beer – the kind that will make your brewing friends grimace and reach for the malt liquor. In fact, many losers have achieved consistently poor results using as few as three of these ten tips.

- **Never Sanitize or Sterilize your Equipment** - Bad beer requires bacteria, wild yeasts and other beasties to produce sour off flavors. Stop all of that unnecessary washing and sanitizing and let your equipment go native. You will save money and precious time. No one likes to clean his or her equipment – so just reuse the rotting gunk from your last batch to spoil your next one.

- **Never Use Brewing Software, Keep Notes or Record Recipes** – Everyone knows that brewing good beer is a matter of pure luck and not repeatable. Who needs a bunch of notes cluttering up the place? If you don't measure anything, never keep any notes and never write down your recipe, then you will always miss your target gravity or volume. Don't use brewing software – that might help you match a particular style or know your color or bitterness in advance. It's much better to find out the sex of the baby after it's born. You can always enter it in whatever style category you feel like the day of the competition. Plus, if you do accidentally make a good batch of beer there is no need to panic. Without a recipe or consistent technique your next batch is certain to be completely different.

- **Store your Ingredients in a Warm, Moist, Sunny place** – Bad beer requires some forethought and planning – you can't just expect to throw something stinky together on the spur of the moment. Prepare first by storing your ingredients in the hot sun, or at least a nice moist corner of the cellar. As I mentioned in the section on hops storage, hops degrade quickly under heat and sunlight leaving a warm skunky smell and flavor in your beer. Malts can't be ignored either – crush your grains several weeks ahead of time so they will oxidize and keep them wet and warm to make sure they spoil before brewing. If you're lucky some mold or weevils will gain a foothold for additional character.

- **Don't Boil – Just Mix and Ferment** – The best brewers boil their entire wort for at least 90 minutes to improve clarity, flavor and beer stability. But stability and clarity are mortal enemies of bad beer – so I think it's best to just dump the ingredients in and mix them for a minute or two over a low flame. Plus if you don't boil you will save precious time and money (no need for a pot!)- just toss the yeast in with some water, malt and sugar and call it a day. Be sure to leave the fermenter open for a while so the wild yeast and bacteria can start souring it. No need to leave anything to chance.

- **Add Low Quality Yeast, or None at All** – Bad beer starts with bad ingredients. Don't stop with just stale malt and hops – add some old dry packet bread yeast. You'll save big dollars over the "winners" who probably purchased high quality liquid yeast packages. Also – never create a yeast starter. Yeast starters give your yeast an unfair head start in the wort, and don't allow for bacteria and wild yeasts to take hold. If you are still producing good beer with low quality yeast, consider using no yeast at all! There are plenty of wild yeasts floating around in the air that are free and guaranteed to make bad beer. The Belgians have known this for hundreds of years, and relied on wild yeast and bacteria in many of their greatest brews.

- **Ferment in a Hot Place** – Yeast prefers cooler fermentation temperatures – usually under 70 degrees F for ales and down in the 50+F range for lagers. If you ferment at higher temperatures you can create undesirable flavors of all kinds. Lagers in particular will suffer from fermenting at excessively high temperatures, so turn up the heat and enjoy!

- **Add Sugar and Lots of It** – Many of us carry fond memories of our first homebrewing kit that came with 3.3 lbs of malt and instructions to add 3-4 pounds of nice white cane sugar. The net result was a beer that tasted like a cross between malt liquor and sour cider. You can get that old cidery flavor once again, and save money on malt by adding pounds of delicious table sugar to your next brew.

- **Bottle and Age Improperly** – Bottle your beer by dropping a bit of sugar in each bottle. This gives you random carbonation. Alternately you can mix a random volume of sugar, though this sometimes results in bottle bombs that can make a mess of your kitchen. Be sure you never measure the sugar by weight or mix the sugar in a separate tank before bottling, as this could give you a consistent carbonation level. Once your beer is bottled, store it in a warm sunny place, ideally in clear bottles as the sunlight and heat will rapidly add off flavors and break down its stability.

- **Compete with Style** – When you compete, the proper attitude is critical to losing. You need to have a losing attitude going into the competition. Remember that the word "contest" is derived from the word "con". Everyone involved is there to cheat you – why else would they volunteer to work on the contest for free? Prepare and present your beer to minimize its appeal. Grouse about everyone and everything you possibly can – complain about the venue, the setup, other competitors, the categories and the rules. It helps if you review the rules and make a list of complaints in advance. Complain about the judges whenever they are around as this will really impress them. A consistent negative attitude will endear you to your fellow competitors, who will no longer be threatened by you. It will also clearly mark you as one of the losers.

- **Never Take Advice** – Brewing advice is worth just what you paid for it – nothing. Do you really believe that brewing experts give away their trade secrets for free? Do you think someone who really knows how to brew would offer it to anyone? No – the secrets of the trade are just that – secrets!

Anything you read in a book, on a discussion forum or especially in an online blog is obviously part of a large right wing (or left wing depending on your political leanings) conspiracy to make you brew bad beer so the "cons" can win the "contests". As a famous old guy once said, "a little education is a dangerous thing." Better to hole up in your fallout shelter and develop your own secret recipes until the Ruskies drop the big one.

And whatever you do - don't listen to anything you read here - especially anything written in this section.

Some Closing Thoughts

Though this book started as a collection of beer articles on my blog, the adventure continues. I add new articles weekly at **blog.beersmith.com**, and also have an email newsletter where you can receive regular articles as well as news about brewing topics of all sorts.

I encourage you to visit **blog.beersmith.com**, sign up for my newsletter and look at our home brewing recipe software package called BeerSmith. In the near future I'm also working on video products and more audio and video content.

Thank you for your time, the steady flow of comments I receive each day, thank you for purchasing this book and happy brewing!

Cheers,

Brad

References

The references used in this book are listed by chapter. Where references are not included, it indicates that the technique or material presented is general knowledge available from multiple sources:

Chapter 1

- Papazian, Charles N. The Complete Joy of Homebrewing, Avon Books, New York, NY, 1984

Chapter 2

- Goldhammer, Ted The Brewer's Handbook, KVP Publishers, Clifton, VA, 1999
- Smith, Bradley J, BeerSmith Grain Listing, http://beersmith.com/GrainList.htm
- Fix, George, An Analysis of Brewing Techniques, Brewers Publications, Colorado, 1997
- Zainasheff, Jamil, "Proper Yeast Pitching Rates", 24 May 2007, http://www.mrmalty.com/pitching.php
- Palmer, John J. How to Brew, Brewers Publications, Boulder, CO, 2006

Chapter 3

- Beer Judge Certification Program, BJCP Style Guide 2008, http://bjcp.org, 2008
- Daniels, Ray, Designing Great Beers, Brewers Publications, Boulder, CO, 1996, 2000
- Goldhammer, Ted The Brewer's Handbook, KVP Publishers, Clifton, VA, 1999
- Morey, Dan A., "Beer's Law", Equation for estimating beer color:

http://www.brewingtechniques.com/brewingtechniques/beerslaw/morey.html

- Papazian, Charles N. The Complete Joy of Homebrewing, Avon Books, New York, NY, 1984
- Tinseth, Glenn, "Glenn's Hop Utilization Numbers", Article on hop utilization: http://www.realbeer.com/hops/research.html
- Schwartz, Ken, "Converting All-Grain Recipes to Extract/Partial Mash", Paper for AHA National Homebrewers Conference, Portland, OR, June 23rd, 1998

Chapter 4

- Papazian, Charles N. The Complete Joy of Homebrewing, Avon Books, New York, NY, 1984
- Palmer, John J. How to Brew, Brewers Publications, Boulder, CO, 2006

Chapter 5

- Garetz, Mark, "How to Get – and Keep – Your Hop's Optimum Value", Brewing Techniques Magazine, Jan/Feb 1994
- Draper, D., "First Wort Hopping", Article available on: http://www.brewery.org/library/1stwort.html
- McKay, Alan, "Hop Back", Bodensatz Brewing, http://www.bodensatz.com
- Million, Donald, "Dry Hopping: Techniques", Brew Your Own Magazine, Sept 2003
- "Hop Growing", Brew Your Own Magazine, Vol 12, No 2, March-April 2008

Chapter 6

- "Batch Sparging", Bay Area Masher's Article, http://www.bayareamashers.org/content/maindocs/BatchSparging.htm
- Patrick Hollingdale, "A Guide to All-Grain Brewing in a Bag", http://aussiehomebrewer.com
- de Jonge, Marc, "Decoction Mashing, A Micro-FAQ", http://hbd.org/brewery/library/DecoctFAQ.html
- Goldhammer, Ted The Brewer's Handbook, KVP Publishers, Clifton, VA, 1999
- Palmer, John J. How to Brew, Brewers Publications, Boulder, CO, 2006
- Fix, George, An Analysis of Brewing Techniques, Brewers Publications, Colorado, 1997
- "Understanding Mash pH", Home Brewing Wiki, http://homebrewtalk.com/wiki
- "Conditioned Milling", Brew Your Own Magazine, March-April 2010
- "Mashing", Wikipedia, http://en.wikipedia.org/wiki/Mashing

Chapter 7

- Dixon, Mike, "Yeast Washing", http://hbd.org/carboy/yeast_washing.htm
- "Yeast Harvesting, Re-Pitching", Article by Wyeast Labs, http://www.wyeastlab.com/com-yeast-harvest.cfm
- Fisher, Joe and Dennis, "Brewing with Honey", Brew Your Own Magazine, Sept 2002
- Randy Mosher, Radical Brewing, Brewer's Publications, Boulder, CO, 2004
- "Krausening", Home Brewing Wiki, http://www.homebrewtalk.com/wiki/index.php/Krausening
- Goldhammer, Ted The Brewer's Handbook, KVP Publishers, Clifton, VA, 1999

Chapter 8

- Goldhammer, Ted <u>The Brewer's Handbook</u>, KVP Publishers, Clifton, VA, 1999
- Papazian, Charlie <u>The Homebrewer's Companion</u>, Avon Books, New York, NY, 1994, p 172
- Palmer, John J. <u>How to Brew</u>, Brewers Publications, Boulder, CO, 2006

Chapter 9

- Beer Judge Certification Program, <u>BJCP Style Guide 2008</u>, http://bjcp.org, 2008
- Daniels, Ray, <u>Designing Great Beers</u>, Brewers Publications, Boulder, CO, 1996, 2000
- "India Pale Ale", Wikipedia, http://en.wikipedia.org/wiki/India_Pale_Ale
- "Stout", Wikipedia, http://en.wikipedia.org/wiki/Irish_stout#Dry_or_Irish_stout
- Zainasheff, Jamil and Palmer, John J. <u>Brewing Classic Styles, 80 Winning Recipes Anyone Can Brew</u>, Brewer's Publications, Boulder, CO, 2007

Chapter 10

- Daniels, Ray, <u>Designing Great Beers</u>, Brewers Publications, Boulder, CO, 1996, 2000
- Beer Judge Certification Program, <u>BJCP Style Guide 2008</u>, http://bjcp.org, 2008
- Lodahl, Martin, "Witbier: Belgian White", Brewing Techniques Magazine, Vol 2, No 4, 1994
- "Trappist Beer", Wikipedia, http://en.wikipedia.org/wiki/Trappist_beer
- "Bock", Wikipedia, http://en.wikipedia.org/wiki/Bock

- Zainasheff, Jamil and Palmer, John J. <u>Brewing Classic Styles, 80 Winning Recipes Anyone Can Brew</u>, Brewer's Publications, Boulder, CO, 2007

Chapter 11

- Daniels, Ray, <u>Designing Great Beers</u>, Brewers Publications, Boulder, CO, 1996, 2000
- Beer Judge Certification Program, <u>BJCP Style Guide 2008</u>, http://bjcp.org, 2008
- Zainasheff, Jamil and Palmer, John J. <u>Brewing Classic Styles, 80 Winning Recipes Anyone Can Brew</u>, Brewer's Publications, Boulder, CO, 2007
- "Cream Ale", Wikipedia, http://en.wikipedia.org/wiki/Cream_ale

Recommended Books

Here are some of the books in my library which I recommend:

Daniels, Ray, <u>Designing Great Beers</u>, Brewer's Publications, Boulder, CO, 1996

Palmer, John J., <u>How to Brew</u>, 3rd edition, Brewer's Publications, Boulder, CO, 2006

Zainasheff, Jamil and Palmer, John J. <u>Brewing Classic Styles</u>, Brewer's Publications, Boulder, CO, 2007

Mosher, Randy, <u>Radical Brewing: </u>Recipes, Brewer's Publications, Boulder, CO, 2004

Index

11152718R0

Made in the USA
Lexington, KY
14 September 2011